The German Theater Today

# THE GERMAN THEATER TODAY

A Symposium

Edited with an Introduction
by LEROY R. SHAW

Published for the Department of Germanic Languages of
THE UNIVERSITY OF TEXAS
by
UNIVERSITY OF TEXAS PRESS, AUSTIN

Library of Congress Catalog Card No. 63-17616
Copyright © 1963 by the University of Texas Press

Manufactured in the United States of America

# Contents

The German Theater Today

# Introduction

The five essays in this volume were presented at the University of Texas on November 27–29, 1961, under the general title "The German Theater Today." The occasion was the third in a series of yearly symposia sponsored by the Department of Germanic Languages to bring an American audience closer to significant areas of German culture.

The innocuous title calls for some explanation. The word *German* equals "German-speaking" and describes an institution that might best be characterized as a peculiar combination of diversity and unity. There are four distinct "German" theaters, an Austrian and a Swiss, a West, and an East German theater, and their national differences are underscored by linguistic tensions that are often rather tricky to define. A German-speaking dramatist, for example, will find it relatively simple to decide between dialect or the standard language as his medium, but he cannot choose to disassociate himself from the cultural-linguistic idiom into which he is born. His work is affected by this circumstance, and local theater repertories often reflect it. Thus the relative absence of a Grillparzer or a Schnitzler on the stages of Hamburg or Frankfurt is not a patriotic snub, but a consequence of paternity, which keeps a playwright from being entirely at home outside his native complex. He *is* played elsewhere, of course, thanks to that official-artificial construction, High German, which provides the German-speaking theater its most potent unifying factor. But on the stage, as on the street, High German is more an act of will than of impulse, an instrument of achievement rather than a source of renewal. Apart from its complete stylization as verse, it derives its life and strength mainly from the speech patterns natural to whoever is using it.

The word *Theater* in the Symposium title implies a similar interplay between the single and the many. Germans often distinguish, for example, between the *Sprechbühne,* a stage on which the text is spoken, and the *Singbühne,* on which the text is sung. Now for most Americans the opera and the stage play are totally unrelated art forms. In the German way of thinking, however, they are simply different species of theater occupying a place side by side on the cultural calendar. The genre distinction is important, but in dramaturgy and criticism, and in the receiving eyes of the public, they are measured by the same theatrical yardstick. Hence the inclusion here of an essay on opera production. Americans should also be aware that the German theater is sharply divided into state-supported and nonstate-supported types. The stability, repertory, and prestige of a stage are all affected by this circumstance; it also fosters a kind of diversity completely unknown in America. Whereas our theater tends to level off into a common denominator, the German-speaking theater prides itself on specialization. The best stages strive for a distinctive and recognizable personality. Their repertory is limited to certain genres; styles of acting and production are developed accordingly; and the ensemble consciously aims at a *niveau* by which their public, and their critics, may always know them.

*Today* in the title has a scholarly as well as a journalistic connotation. The speakers in Austin were dealing with the German-speaking theater now, as it currently exists, but they were also talking about that theater in the present era as a phenomenon with an immediate past and future. Perhaps a touch of the German word *aktuell* has also crept into this "today," to suggest a newsworthy subject, one that is alive, significant, and pertinent at this date. A few weeks before the Texas Symposium, and quite independently of it, another meeting dealing with the theater took place at Bregenz, Austria, with the imposing theme: "The Human Image and Styles of Production in the World Theater in the Atomic Age [*Menschenbild und Inszenierungsformen des Welttheaters im Atomzeitalter*]." The Bregenz Symposium was addressed to a public acquainted with the German-speaking theater at first hand. Speakers there had come to review the traditional notions of theater and to re-examine its functions in the light of this hectic age. Consequently, at Bregenz the sense of immediacy was prominent, the relationship between life and the theater was taken for granted, and the evaluation of specific contemporary conditions was freely and frankly rendered. Yet in spite of these differences the two meetings were in many respects astonishingly alike. Their realization of *Aktualität,* for example, began with interpreting the concept "today" in terms of its spatial as well as its temporal dimensions. The participants in both symposia came from widely divergent regions of the theater world. They are of different nationality, they hold different positions in or outside the system, and they approach it from various points of view.

The lectures of the Texas Symposium are reproduced here in the sequence in which they were presented. Although not deliberate, the arrangement shows a happy symmetry. The series opened and closed with representatives of two extremes of the modern German theater, Wagner and Brecht, both of them creators of words for music, the one an illusionist now under trial, the other an anti-illusionist open to doubt from many an angle. The second and fourth lectures were concerned with the problem of transference: the reception of American drama on the German stage, and conversely, the introduction of German drama in America. The third lecture stands as a kind of informational interlude, a broad survey of the theater as a cultural institution, providing a needed vantage point for those who are not already reasonably well acquainted with the field.

The series was opened by A. M. Nagler, professor of dramatic history and criticism at the Yale University School of Drama. "Wagnerian Productions in Postwar Bayreuth" gives a glimpse of German theater from a discipline so little known in English there is not even a name for it. Literally, *Theaterwissenschaft* is "science of the theater," an expression unnatural to us, since it assumes a definable object of study not yet recognized as such in this country. Professor Nagler argues a simple but forthright point: that the Bayreuth productions under Wagner's grandsons have rejected the decorative, theater-oriented musical drama in favor of the sparse, abstract, antitheater oratorio. The implications of this development—and Professor Nagler's dispassionate argument does not entirely shy away from them—are enormously important to the future of the German theater. At issue, for example, and now hotly debated in theater journals, is the determination of artistic policy. Without a doubt, the director nowadays has come to exercise an influence far beyond his basic function. Seniority, talent, or extra-artistic considerations (all of them applicable to Wagner's grandsons) may turn that influence into seeming indispensability. And indispensability, so runs the thesis of the detractors, soon leads to omnipotence, which in its turn extends to omnipresence as well, especially when the director is invited to carry out his idea in theaters other than his own. The result is increasing standardization, with respect to any individual work, about what is "right" for the theater as a whole. All of this is in direct contradiction to the artistic diversity that has long been the system's greatest source of strength.

The controversy over Wagner productions also stirs up the old problem of maintaining a balance between the forces of tradition and the forces of innovation. In the German-speaking theater, as Dr. Schlag points out, experimentation as such belongs primarily to the private, or little, theater, the so-called *Kellerbühne*. Yet the state-supported theaters also live with this struggle for balance and have to resolve it in their own way. On the one hand, their problem is taking issue with the classics, of deciding how Wagner (or Shakespeare or Schiller) is to be staged and interpreted now; on the other hand, it is a problem of keeping the repertory sound, of providing a healthy proportion of foreign and native plays, of modern and classic works. This problem is not apt to get any simpler. Today there is not only an increasing number of original and worthwhile German plays, there is also a growing clamor to see good works of the recent past that have not yet had their day on the contemporary stage.

Finally Professor Nagler's lecture hints at a theoretical issue suggested again by the provocative title of the last lecture, "Epic Theater Is Lyric Theater." In its simplest form this question concerns the nature of the art forms now being presented. Is a Wagner work presented as oratorio still a Wagnerian opera? Is an epic play (to say nothing of an epic-lyric play) still a drama? And in interpretations of the classics, it becomes doubtful whether these works are given in the form for which they basically exist. Are contemporary audiences all too often being tricked into accepting a subtle perversion of the real thing, a surrogate that is no substitute? Closely related to such questions is the possibility that the theater is no longer true to its own nature. The Bregenz Symposium was much concerned with this lack of fidelity, notably in the lecture by Fritz Hochwälder, one of Austria's better modern dramatists. He deplores the loss of *Naivität,* that sense of play for the sake of play, of spontaneous participation by playwright, public, and player in a serious dialectical game; and its replacement by too much self-consciousness, through which word and gesture have become literature and dramatic dynamics solely a working-out of ideas. At its worst, according to Hochwälder, the theater today has become "an arena for intellectual jugglers."

With the second essay, "American Drama and the German Stage," the series moves from the careful world of the *Theaterwissenschaftler* into the excitement of the first-nighter. As drama critic and coeditor of the Berlin newspaper *Der Tagesspiegel* Walther Karsch is a past master at interpreting today's news for tomorrow's readers. Yet even as Professor Nagler discovers *Aktualität* from his historical lookout, so does Mr. Karsch gain insight into a piece of history through a survey of the changing fortunes of American drama on the German stage. Whether speaking privately or for all intelligent German playgoers, Mr. Karsch broadly views the ranks of modern American playwrights, with Tennessee Williams and Arthur Miller doing rather badly, William Inge and Edward Albee slightly better, Thornton Wilder and Eugene O'Neill excellently. The ranking itself is interesting; the reasoning behind it even more so. Wilder and O'Neill are praised, not as one might expect, for their ability to present the American Way of Life, nor even for their influence on the contemporary German theater, but for qualities Mr. Karsch unashamedly calls poetic strength, love of theater, and striving for universal significance. Now whatever we may think of these characteristics as a basis for judging plays—and pragmatic American tastes might well be somewhat suspicious— we note with satisfaction that these are the standards of a daily reviewer. A theater with such critical guardians may not always be a happy one, but it is fortunate, for here the everyday is gauged according to history and the judgment of an individual work is made against the background of world drama.

The third lecture of the series, "Thespian Austria," was given by Dr. Wilhelm Schlag, cultural affairs officer for the Austrian Consulate General in New York. Although based on Austrian conditions, this survey of the theater as a cultural institution suggests many of the problems faced by the German-speaking theater elsewhere. Dr. Schlag touches upon two points that were of central interest at the Bregenz Symposium. One concerns the effect upon the theater of general economic conditions. Without a doubt, the German-speaking theater has profited enormously from the free flow of money in present-day Europe: new houses have been built and old ones renovated; personnel has increased and its competitive position has been recognized; the state generously supports its own theater and the houses are sold out nightly. Yet the speakers at Bregenz were less concerned with loss of self-control in the face of the economic miracle than with the possibility that the theater itself had become a kind of *Wirtschaftswunder*. "With its huge external expenditures, the German stage has become a true reflection of the economic miracle which does not satisfy the soul." Hochwälder's words remind us of what we have often heard about our own Broadway. There is no lack of things to buy in today's theatrical supermarket, but the foodstuffs are without substance. They increase the appetite without nourishing the man.

A charge of this gravity obviously springs from a conviction that the theater has a social, or even moral function in addition to its role as entertainer. The Bregenz speakers insisted upon this point. In Heinz Kindermann's words, the theater is "one of the most significant institutions for self-knowledge . . . , an organ of self-confirmation amidst the confusions that undermine one's self-confidence." For Heinz Beckmann, every visit to the theater is a moral experience. "The human being who encounters himself there . . . acquires at least a vague notion of his existence within a larger context and in another perspective than his ordinary, everyday one." At Bregenz, then, it was agreed that the theater does not merely *reproduce* reality, but that it *mirrors* it in *counterreflection;* the playgoer is forced to compare his own picture of himself, and of his world, with the image given him on the stage. In short, by going to the theater he declares his willingness to undergo an act of moral contemplation. The theater's failure to provide opportunity for this experience is a denial of its justification for being, which no expenditure of time or money can long hide. Hence Hochwälder's diagnosis that the German-speaking theater today is "an organism suspiciously like a sun-browned tubercular patient; he looks full of life, but is already halfway in the grave."

The strongest institutions, like the most reliable individuals, have usually been aware of their own weaknesses. Thus the soul-searching at Bregenz may also be read as a declaration of strength. In fact, it seems almost American in its troubled dissatisfaction with things as they are, and this precisely at the moment when they seem to have arrived at a peak of achievement. To this somewhat unexpected similarity between the German-speaking and the English-speaking situations, one might add another, rather more direct common element suggested by the statistics in Dr. Schlag's essay. As we know, the German-speaking theater is predominantly a state-supported, *repertoire* theater; it has a resident ensemble and presents a limited number of plays with premières and performances scattered throughout the season. Ours is largely a private, *en suite* theater; various, unrelated houses offer a single play, with a cast specifically hired for the purpose, as long as there is a paying audience or an available star. This is not the place to argue the merits of either system, and they were not discussed at the Austin or the Bregenz meetings. It seems possible, however, that the *en suite* theater in German-speaking countries may be gaining ground, not in the state-supported system, but in the growing number of private theaters. The proportion of *en suite* to *repertoire* houses in München, for example, is now about two to one. This tendency —if it is that— is doubly interesting because the opposite may be taking place in the United States. A number of cities now have foundation-supported or municipally maintained houses of the highest quality; repertory groups, whether stationary or travelling, are on the rise; and the projected *repertoire* theater in New York's Lincoln Center opens under highest patronage as a model for the rest of the country. In this connection, German newspapers recently reported with obvious pleasure Arthur Miller's hope that the repertory idea would enliven the American theater and revive our former tradition.

The American and the German-speaking theaters are both showing considerable interest today in the educative function. Dr. Schlag mentions Austria's Theater der Jugend, which not only seeks out new audiences where none existed before, but also aims at developing the public's potential for receiving and comprehending the theater's storehouse of treasures. Developments of this sort are relatively new in the German-speaking countries; they have long been with us in the shape of the educational theater. University and college drama departments have come indeed to exercise more and more influence on America's theater life, both in creating an intelligent audience and in supplying future playwrights, actors, directors, and designers for the professional stage. The educational theater, especially in its relationship to German drama, is the subject of the fourth essay, "German Drama and the American Stage," by Professor Francis Hodge of the University of Texas Department of Drama.

Professor Hodge's place among the Symposium lecturers is unique. By his own confession, he is "not an authority on German theater or drama." On the other hand, he alone of the participants is actually engaged with the stage, and he belongs among the pioneers of German epic theater in America with his productions of Brecht's *Mother Courage* and *The Good Woman of Setzuan* on the University of Texas stage. It was said that Professor Hodge's subject offers the counterpart to Mr. Karsch's. Yet there are deeply-lying differences. Mr. Karsch reports on a situation of plenty, in which every American play of any significance, and many more besides, have had a chance upon the German stage. He is able to evaluate that situation as a piece of contemporary history. Professor Hodge, on the contrary, is talking about a period in which very few German plays have reached the American theater public. His inquiry concerns the meaning of a history that has not taken place. Mr. Karsch, furthermore, encounters his subject as a finished thing: the play has been adapted and performed; his is the task of judging what has been done. Professor Hodge for his part always faces a problem as well as a potential: the plays are there; what must be done to adapt, prepare, and perform them for American reception? The problem of transference, which was touched upon in previous essays as a German problem, appears here in fullest *Aktualität* as a matter for our specific attention. In effect, Professor Hodge's lecture throws out a series of challenges to American laymen and professionals alike. The speaker and student of German is challenged to provide translations and to consider how he might spread his knowledge of German theater within the limited circles open to him. The professional is challenged to measure his background against the foreign scene and to speculate upon the sources still untapped by the American theater. And the ordinary playgoer is challenged to reflect upon the nature of his theatrical experience and to ask himself whether he is being given all that the theater has to offer him.

Throwing out challenges, and meeting them, has been a lifelong activity of the fifth speaker at the Texas Symposium. Eric Bentley, professor of dramatic art at Columbia University, has played many variations on his basic role as propagator for the European theater in America. He has appeared variously—and at times simultaneously, with a skill approaching legerdemain—as critic, reviewer, director, translator-adapter, poet, and cultural ambassador without portfolio. To cap this versatility, he appeared before us as a theater performer in the mask of the cabaret artist, singing and playing and commenting upon his own performance.

Typically, Professor Bentley prefers to demonstrate rather than theorize, and in his address he does not expatiate on the implications of "Epic Theater Is Lyric Theater." No doubt he would agree that the theory of epic theater, as Hochwälder remarked at the Bregenz Symposium, "is neither right nor wrong, but on the one hand useful and necessary, on the other harmful or super-fluous. For Brecht it was useful inasmuch as it allowed him not only to hide the specific weaknesses of his dramatic gift, but to turn them to good advantage; it is harmful inasmuch as it can be used by others in the belief that plays can be written with its help." Brecht's cavalier attitude to his own brainchild is well illustrated by the anecdote of the one-time coworker who came to him with a new play, insisting it had been written according to the rules. Brecht allegedly replied: "But for heaven's sake, man, the theory is false!"

Now Professor Bentley is far too shrewd a man to take every utterance of the master at face value. Furthermore, his knowledge that language, not theory, is the instrument by which a poet trans-forms life into art results in his imaginative use of Brecht's own lyrics to tell the story of a life in which all events, the doubtful and the corruptible not excluded, have been turned by the mysteri-ous inner workings of language into unmistakable and incorrupti-ble art. And the relationship of such lyric-epic to the theater? It lies in realizing the three qualities mentioned by Hochwälder as essential for living theater: a language "universally understood, simple, unadorned, direct"; the attitude of *Naivität*, with its freedom from psychological complexities and its unadulterated pleasure in play; and the possession of conscience, which holds the mirror up to a spectator so that he is forced to take issue with himself, "his heart being purified without himself being changed."

If this last expression sounds paradoxical, even perverse, it is because the theater itself exhibits perversity as an institution that can realize itself only by doing the opposite of what it purports to accomplish. Within the narrow dimensions of a stage it presents the whole world, through the medium of play it demonstrates the seriousness of life, in the telling of lies it reveals the truth, and in the indulgence of pitiless amorality it deepens the moral sense. The theater is possibly the only art form that creates while it interprets, sings without music and speaks without words, discovers its own individuality through association with other genres, and finds its independence through dependency—for without its actors to enact and its audience to react, the presentation would not otherwise exist.

We return then to the description with which we began, of an institution both unified and diverse, one and many, unique and eclectic. The German-speaking theater springs from this ambivalence. Accordingly we understand the conglomeration of themes at the Texas Symposium, with its emphasis on the problem of transfer; and we understand the sweeping evaluations, for good and bad, at the meeting in Bregenz. The theater, in fact, *demands* judgment of its mediations: between tradition and vision, artist and public, modes and genuine styles, above all, according to its skill in suffusing the local with the international, the native with the foreign, for its greatest glory is a *völkerverbindende Mission*, the task of making a diverse world aware of its oneness.

LEROY R. SHAW

Austin, Texas

Wagnerian Productions in Postwar Bayreuth

A. M. NAGLER

# Wagnerian Productions in Postwar Bayreuth

A. M. NAGLER

Bayreuth is a city of some fifty thousand inhabitants, not far from Nuremberg and only a short distance from the Czechoslovakian border. Here in the rural environment of the Franconian hills Richard Wagner selected a spot on which to build his Festival Playhouse as a shrine where pilgrims were expected to experience the most authentic productions of Wagnerian music drama, originally staged by the High Priest himself.

Wagner had composed his tetralogy *The Ring of the Nibelung* especially for Bayreuth, and the Festival Theater was opened in 1876 with a performance of the cycle. Wagner's last opera, *Parsifal,* likewise had its first production in Bayreuth (1882). After Wagner's death in 1883 most of his earlier operas were incorporated into the Bayreuth *repertoire*. The enterprise was kept going first by Wagner's widow, Cosima, then by his son Siegfried and his daughter-in-law. Since the end of World War II Richard Wagner's grandchildren, Wieland and Wolfgang, are in command at Bayreuth, where during the past decade they have staged a series of sensational productions. Before explaining the nature of the sensation I should like to give you some data concerning the physical plant.

The Festival Playhouse was built by Otto Brückwald, in part after plans which Gottfried Semper had worked out for a projected Wagnerian Festival Theater at Munich. Semper, Brückwald, and Wagner developed a rising wedge-shaped amphitheater of the Grecian type. At the lower edge of the wedge lies the picture-frame stage, clearly a compromise solution. The capacity of the house is 1,860. The proscenium opening measures 38 x 36 feet (12.75 x 12 m.); the actual width of the stage is 63 feet (21 m.); and the depth is 75 feet (25 m.) from the footlights. If the rear of the stage is included, the maximum depth amounts to 114 feet (38 m.). The traproom has a height of some 30 feet. The height of the stage to the flyloft is 90 feet. In the back is a huge cyclorama. The Bayreuth stage boasts of its very advanced lighting equipment. For the production of *Tannhäuser* in 1955, for instance, 290 separate units (not counting the footlights) were used in conjunction with 40 projectors; experimental use was made of 2 xenon lamps. By 1960 Bayreuth used xenon lamps exclusively, and last year's *Ring* was lit with 17 xenon lamps and additional xenon projectors.

The orchestra pit is sunk and invisible to the audience. Between the first row of seats and the footlights are no distracting lights, no conductor sawing the air with his arms, no visible musicians. This dark region has become the magic abyss from which the music emanates like the Pythian vapors in the Delphic shrine.

When Wagner first staged *The Ring of the Nibelung* in Bayreuth (1876) he adopted the type of stage he was conversant with, the stage of his period, equipped with a painted backdrop, painted wings and borders, and strewn with painted set pieces. In short, Wagner's production style was representational, realistic in terms of the painted stage. A look at Josef Hoffmann's *Ring* designs (executed in the Brückner Studio at Coburg) gives us a pretty good idea of the appearance of the Bayreuth stage in 1876 during Acts I and III of *Die Walküre*. In 1882 Paul Joukowsky was responsible for the *Parsifal* designs, and those who remembered his

18

Temple of the Holy Grail or his set for the first scene of Act III were quite enthusiastic about the glow of these décors as long as they were illuminated by gas light. (Later on, electric light brought on a harshness which destroyed the remote mystery of the original concept.)

In 1882 a visitor came to Bayreuth who was not at all impressed by Joukowsky's gas-lit magic. The spectator was Adolphe Appia, a Swiss artist who was shocked by the illusionistic style of the Wagnerian productions, by the literalness with which Wagner's stage directions had been carried out. On his drawing board Appia, a true connoisseur of Wagner's music, had envisaged a quite different setting for the Wagnerian music drama. In his designs Appia wanted to liberate the cluttered stage from the jumble of factual detail. He intended to replace all this with semi-abstract plastic settings which were to be made expressive of the developing dramatic action by the use of colored light. The flat painted canvasses were to be discarded in favor of three-dimensional set pieces which were to be lighted in an expressive way in accordance with the emotional fluctuations of the music. Appia was the discoverer of the expressive potentialities of electric light, and he used floodlighting and spotlights as a means of altering his three-dimensional sets in tune with the score and the development of the dramatic action.

Take the second act of *Tristan*. The stage direction asks for a garden set at night with the entrance to a castle lit by a lonely burning torch. This is the place where Isolde is to meet her Tristan. By extinguishing the torch she is to give him the signal that he may come since her husband has left for a hunt. Here is Appia's interpretation: "When Isolde enters, she is conscious of only two facts, Tristan's absence and the torch which separates her from Tristan. Isolde is no longer aware of the warm summer night that envelops the tall trees in the park. To her these distances are nothing but the terrifying emptiness which separates her from Tristan . . . In extinguishing the torch she removes this barrier. She wipes out the hostile space, and time comes to a stop. Time and space, the natural environment, the sinister torch have ceased to exist, for Tristan is now in Isolde's arms . . . And we experience, with the hero and heroine, nothing else but their ecstatic union. Their soul-stirring passion appears to us, as to them, much more real than their bodily presence." Only once did Appia have the opportunity of seeing his *Tristan* designs executed, and that was in 1923 when Toscanini invited him to stage the work at La Scala, Milan. Bayreuth showed no interest in Appia during the lifetime of the artist, who died in 1928. In the 1930's, however, the Appian spirit began to make itself felt on the Bayreuth stage in visually superb productions of the *Ring,* designed by Emil Preetorius.

This much for the background. Let us now turn to the postwar performances in Bayreuth.

On July 30, 1951, a performance of *Parsifal* opened the first postwar festival cycle in Bayreuth. Wieland Wagner's stage was practically empty. The spectators were confronted with a disk which remained onstage through all the scenes. In Act I light seeping through the gauze curtain in the rear suggested trees. Later, tables were set on the disk for the Knights of the Holy Grail. The Flowermaidens made their abortive attempts at seducing Parsifal on the disk, and in the last act Kundry was baptized on it. The required scene changes were executed by light, although a few set pieces were brought in, a seat for Gurnemanz or Amfortas and the tables for the Knights. Projections on a scrim were used for Act II, Scene I, to display a sort of spiderweb design in which Kundry seemed to be caught by the wiles of the magician Klingsor and, shortly thereafter, to soften the contours of the Flowermaiden scene. A mystic semidarkness hovered over everything. During the Good Friday Spell the disk received a projected greenish-yellowish hue with interspersed light spots, but the color of the disk did not keep pace with the radiance emanating from the orchestra pit.

In 1951 *Parsifal* was followed by Wieland Wagner's new *Ring* cycle, a production which he kept in the festival program for eight consecutive summers, making changes every year but retaining his basic pattern after 1953, when he put the action on a disk which, in combination with projections, dominated all the scenes in the annual *Ring* productions from 1953 through 1958.

It cannot be my task here to record the various changes and

their dates. A few examples must suffice. In his first *Ring*, of 1951, Wieland Wagner had certain set pieces on his stage. Some scenes even had a conventional quality, such as Hunding's hut in *Die Walküre*, Act I. By 1955 the walls of the hut had disappeared, and the stage was dominated by a stylized tree. In 1957 a triangular structure of beams was thrown around the tree. I mention the three solutions because they show how Wieland Wagner, when dissatisfied with one attempt, works out another and still a third. The subsequent solutions are not necessarily improvements, but there is no air of finality in present-day Bayreuth.

The second act of *Siegfried* has also undergone several changes. In 1951 a tree and some foliage were still in evidence. A year later, the scene had become abstract. The dragon Fafner made his farewell appearance in 1952, and since then only puffs of smoke betray the presence of Siegfried's adversary. By 1957 the second act had an almost Appian quality, and the visual analogue to the forest murmurs in the orchestra consisted of the green color that was projected onto the disk and the framing steps. Wieland Wagner stages some of the most impressive moments in the *Ring* with the help of projections on the naked disk: the opening scene of *Götterdämmerung*, for instance, with the three Teutonic Parcae twisting the fateful rope and the electrical storm pattern projected on a scrim, or the clouds moving over the heads of the Valkyries, or the awakening of Brünnhilde on top of the rock.

No *Ring* performances were scheduled for 1959. In 1960 a new *Ring* was designed and staged by Wolfgang Wagner. This time, the unifying gimmick in the performances of the cycle was a concave disk, a sort of circular platter, which signified the world. The disk, with a diameter of forty-five feet, could be divided into five segments. As long as the gods and semi-gods behaved, the disk remained whole. But then Alberich stole the gold from the bottom of the Rhine, and Wotan committed one crime after another. By the time we reached *Die Walküre*, the disk was broken, and its segments were arranged in various combinations. The world was literally out of joint. At the end of the tetralogy, when the ring had reverted to the Rhine-maidens and Walhalla was enveloped in purifying flames, the disk became one again, *à vista*, signifying the dawn of a new day. Only a few set pieces were used in the course

21

of the cycle: an anvil for Mime, a shaky castle for Gunther, the bottom of the Rhine, a reef for the gold. In most of the scenes, however, the designer-director achieved the desired effects with his disk segments and projections. Unforgettable was the projected rainbow bridge that rolled onto the stage like a carpet fit for the gods to tread upon.

Wieland Wagner is not a determined theoretician. Consequently, he has not issued any lengthy manifestoes. But he has made a few pronouncements, mainly stressing the symbolic aspects of this or that Wagnerian opera, and he has brought to the attention of the readers of the Bayreuth program brochures a few utterances which Richard Wagner had made and in which he was quoted as having expressed his dismay over the limitations of the contemporary stage. On one occasion Richard Wagner recorded his discomfiture by wishing, after he had solved the problem of the invisible orchestra, that he could also invent the "invisible theater." In a letter to King Ludwig II he expressed his sense of frustration in the following words: "Everyone thinks he can outdo me by better and more beautiful things while I am only striving for . . . a certain poetic effect, but no theatrical pomp. Scenery, for instance, is invariably designed as though it were to be looked at for its own sake, as in a panorama. But I want only a subdued background to characterize a dramatic situation."

It appears to me, however, a rash assumption that Richard Wagner suffered under the medium he had to work with. When he created his operas he composed them very much for the stage form of his day: the gaslit wing-and-border stage behind a proscenium frame. By conducting in various opera houses, Wagner had acquired a thorough knowledge of staging conditions on the picture-frame stage. The painted stage of illusion was his domain, and he never demanded more (or less, for that matter) of the scenic artist than his painterly illusionism was able to achieve on the stage. And when the German painters were not good enough, he suggested that Parisian painters be put to work. And when he could not expect to get a "lifelike" dragon from German craftsmen, he sent to England for a realistic replica of a monster with glowing eyes, jaws which would open, and nostrils emitting smoke. Wagner simply was not satisfied with mere puffs of smoke from an imagined monster behind a rocky set piece.

When *Tannhäuser* had its first night in Dresden (1845) Wagner persuaded the management to order the scenery from Paris. The composer had been very much impressed by the work of the Parisian scene painters, and when he compared their products with the work of their German colleagues, the Parisian sets appeared to him as "true and noble works of art." The Dresden intendant yielded to Wagner's request, and the sets for the first *Tannhäuser* were imported from Paris. They were manufactured in the studio of the famous E. D. J. Despléchin. The Parisian set for the Venusberg did not please Wagner, and the local scene painter in Dresden had to do a little retouching. But the valley of the Wartburg in the sunlight of a May day was, in Wagner's words, "a complete success." The hall in the castle arrived too late for opening night, and the hall of Charles V from Weber's *Oberon* was pressed into service as a substitute. But for the second performance the Despléchin interior of the Wartburg was on the boards, and Wagner was so delighted with it that he advised the managers of other theaters to copy the Parisian set for future productions of *Tannhäuser*. The third act of the opera requires the same setting as Act I, Scene 2, but with this difference: it is now autumn, and the yellow leaves on the trees and on the ground are symbolic of Tannhäuser's tragedy. In Wagnerian opera nature always plays an important role, painted nature, to be sure, yet nature with an emotional ring. The Dresden management had thought that money could be saved by simply using the spring décor of Act I, Scene 2, for Act III. But this did not work. Dimming the lights was not sufficient; the spring set remained a spring set and refused to become a fall décor. Wagner insisted that in future productions the set for Act III be expressly painted in autumnal colors.

You gather from all this that Wagner did not think in terms of "invisible theater." He was a neurotic in many other respects, but lived in harmony with the painted stage, provided the painting was done by an artist who knew his craft.

Illusionistic realism was the principle which Wagner applied also to his handling of the chorus and the supernumeraries. The entrance of the guests into the Wartburg hall is an example. Wagner wanted to have this action executed "in an arrangement which would mirror real life." He wrote: "Let's do away with the embarrassing regularity which we find in the traditional marching procedure. The entrance of the guests is bound to appear more pleasing to the eye if the guests come in in varied and casual groups, divided into families and friends." And during the singers' contest he again asked for a "casual grouping and for variation in the facial expressions as the listeners [on the stage] follow the unfolding action." Wagner continues: "These are the moments when the stage director has a chance to shine . . . In the same spirit he has to direct the pilgrims in Acts I and III; casualness and naturalness must determine the groupings if my intention is to be realized." When Wagner wrote the stage directions at the end of Act I, where the hunters should come in with their game, their dogs, and the horses, he really meant it; he believed in this "slice of [medieval] life." This becomes clear from his complaint against the Dresden production: "In view of the fact that our ordinary supernumeraries are stiff and self-conscious, I was not able to achieve the overwhelming gaiety of this scene."

Wagner was interested in the imitation of an action. To him drama was mimesis. What he understood by imitation is clearly set forth in his stage directions: spring painted on canvas, irregular stragglers on their pilgrimage to Rome, the shepherd boy playing his shawm, the falling leaves, the evening star, the torches of the funeral procession, the dogs and horses—all this was imitation of an action. In addition the singing actor is called upon to react, in gestures and facial expressions, to the subtlest suggestions of the orchestra as Wagner had demanded of his Vienna Tannhäuser, Schnorr von Carolsfeld. Wagner once described his coaching method, how, during a rehearsal, he would stand next to the singer whispering to him what *must* go on in the mind and soul of Tannhäuser as he stands there released from the bondage of Frau Venus, slowly finding his way back to humanity.

With this background material in mind let us now turn to Wieland Wagner's Bayreuth production of *Tannhäuser* in 1955. For this opera the stage floor consisted of a raked plane fifty-four feet wide and sixty-three feet deep. In Act II the depth was increased by nine feet. The slope was rather marked as the stage rose eight feet over a distance of sixty-three. For Act I, Scene 1, the grotto of Venus, the stage floor was covered with a purple ground cloth. The "scenery" consisted of semielliptical ornaments, the first six made of gold-plated wire, those in the back being projections. The spiral on the ground was likewise projected. In this abstract space the Bacchanale was staged as an orgy of sex with an interlude of two solo dancers miming the act of cohabitation.

From the Venus grotto the scene changes *à vista* to the valley of the Wartburg. But in Bayreuth there was no Wartburg, no valley, no blue sky. Instead, Wieland Wagner had hit upon the idea of borrowing from medieval miniatures the gold background with six golden wings on either side of the stage. Five stylized trees were added, and far downstage there rose a black cross, edged with white, to a height of forty feet. The stage was now covered with a light green ground cloth, on which white spots were projected— just a touch of spring. One enthusiastic critic felt that this was sufficient as long as the golden background, reminiscent of illuminated manuscripts, preserved "the unity of the patterned medieval philosophy of life [*die Einheit des gebundenen mittelalterlichen Lebensgefühls*] as it should be expressed here." Should this really be expressed? How meaningless a reference to the medieval philosophy of life! We are not dealing with the poems of Hartmann von der Aue or Walther von der Vogelweide, but with Wagner's *Tannhäuser*. Let us consider for a moment the dramatic situation. The hero is standing before us, freed from the shackles of Venus, he is quite *entbunden,* and through a miracle of faith restored to humanity and nature. The echoes of Tannhäuser's hymn to Venus have died away, and we are getting set for the singer's jubilant paean to spring and all that it entails in terms of love and human relations. And let us listen to the music; it is romantic music, a music full of drive and sap and bursting buds. Who is willing to think here of illuminated medieval codices? By ignoring Wagner's stage directions, by distorting his intentions, you may be able to express all sorts of hidden meanings, but you are likely to do violence to what emerges from the score for the normal listener who simply surrenders to the irrational emotional elements that arise from the orchestra pit.

One other observation concerning Act I, Scene 2. Wieland Wagner's chorus of Old Pilgrims comes in, eighty men, all in black, all with the same hair style, all marching in one rhythm. No "natural grouping" such as Richard Wagner had postulated. Instead, a sort of Grecian chorus in rank and file. Later, at the end of Act I, the composer had asked for the bustle of hunters, dogs, and horses, whereas the grandson introduced here a formal grouping of a train of sixty-two hunters in red uniforms.

In Act II the Bayreuth chorus enters likewise in marching formation. Everything about the Wartburg is highly stylized and formal. The guests move in *en bloc,* the men in one uniform costume, the women in another. The six contestants also wear one type of costume, only Tannhäuser, the nonconformist, is singled out by a red sash. He is in opposition (so goes the official symbolic interpretation) to a stereotyped, rigid courtly society that is unable to understand the ecstasy of love. Hence their marionettelike movements on the checkerboard pattern that marks the floor of the hall, defined as such by the Romanesque arches and the benches along the side walls, where the men sit on one side and the women on the other.

In the last act Bayreuth showed again the darkened space of Act I, Scene 2, though the stylized trees had now lost their foliage. When Venus reappears, the elliptical forms come back. A spotlight focuses on the dying protagonist. The Young Pilgrims do not march in, but appear instead in a sort of glowing pyramid, and with this apotheosis we are in the midst of an outright oratorio.

In his production Wieland Wagner wanted to raise the specific case of Tannhäuser to universal significance—the instance of the man torn between sensuality and spirituality at last finding redemption in woman's sacrifice and self-denial. But if my memory is correct, this message was obvious in all previous productions I have seen, productions far removed from the form of scenic oratorio.

Wieland Wagner's *mise en scène* for *Lohengrin* was another attempt to turn romantic opera into a static scenic oratorio. The arrival of Lohengrin may serve to illustrate the hieratic production style of 1958. When the Swan Knight arrives, the Wagnerian chorus (and I mean Richard Wagner's) gets very excited. Every-

Bayreuth, 1882. *Parsifal*, Act III

Design by Paul von Joukowsky. Photograph: Festspiele Bayreuth. Copyright: Festspielleitung Bayreuth.

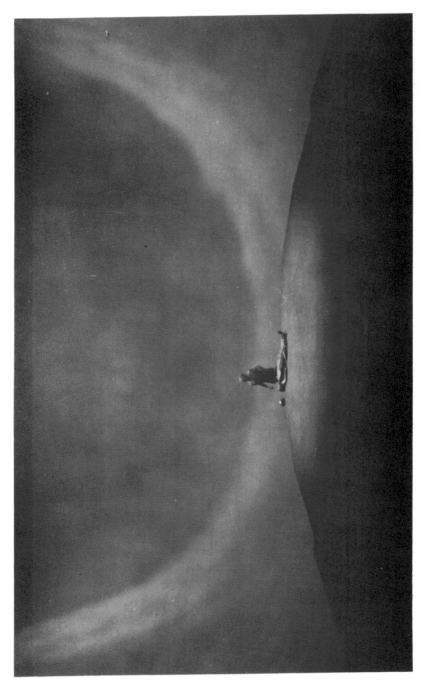

Bayreuth, 1952. *Siegfried*, Act III

Design by Wieland Wagner. Photograph: Festspiele Bayreuth—Schwennicke. Copyright: Festspielleitung Bayreuth.

Bayreuth, 1955. *Parsifal*, Act I

Design by Wieland Wagner. Photograph: Festspiele Bayreuth—Lauterwasser. Copyright: Festspielleitung Bayreuth.

Bayreuth, 1955. *Parsifal*, Act III
Design by Wieland Wagner. Photograph: Festspiele Bayreuth. Copyright:
Festspielleitung Bayreuth.

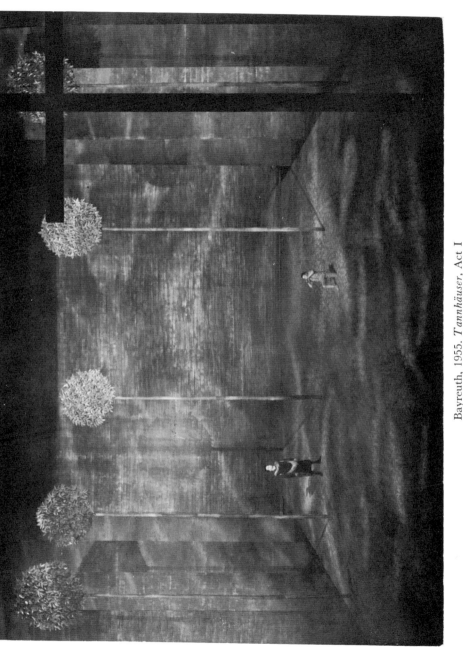

Bayreuth, 1955. *Tannhäuser*, Act I

Design by Wieland Wagner. Photograph: Festspiele Bayreuth—Lauterwasser. Copyright: Festspielleitung Bayreuth.

Bayreuth, 1955. *Tannhäuser*, Act II

Design by Wieland Wagner. Photograph. Festspiele Bayreuth. Lastenzauren. Copyright. Festspielhäuser, Bayreuth.

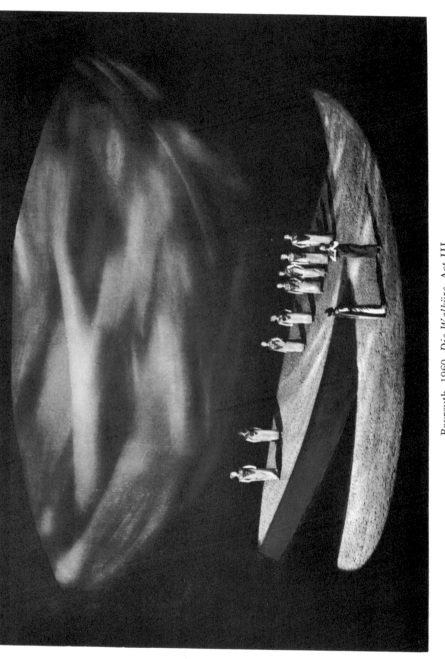

Bayreuth, 1960. *Die Walküre*, Act III

Design by Wolfgang Wagner. Photograph: Festspiele Bayreuth—Lauterwasser. Copyright: Festspielleitung Bayreuth.

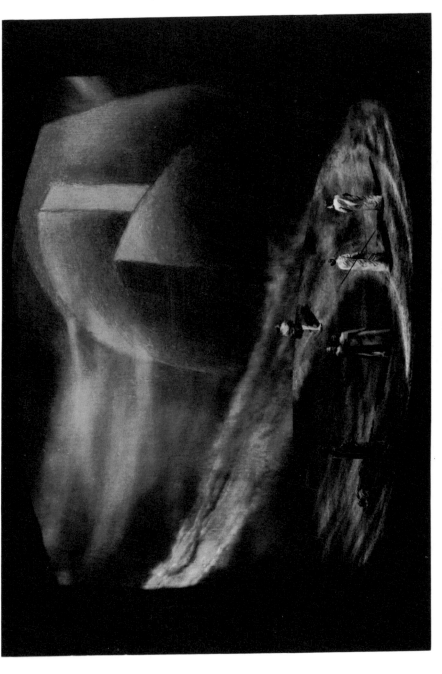

Bayreuth, 1960. *Das Rheingold*, Scene IV

Design by Wolfgang Wagner. Photograph: Festspiele Bayreuth—Lauterwasser. Copyright: Festspielleitung Bayreuth.

body rushes to the bank of the river expressing amazement at the arrival of a knight in shining armor, standing in a boat drawn by a swan. The male chorus is divided into two half choruses until their voices merge in the assertion that a miracle has taken place before their eyes.

In Wieland Wagner's production the choristers sing the music which the grandfather had written, highly emotional and dramatic music, and they sing it to perfection. But the chorus does not show any outward signs of emotion. The members of the chorus are posted on the steps of an amphitheater and remain in this position, hardly ever lifting an arm, throughout the entire first act. Lohengrin arrives, but the chorus does not even bother to look at him, nor does Elsa for that matter. Nor does she kneel before Lohengrin after he has addressed her, and Lohengrin is not given a chance to embrace her. The spectator has, from the very beginning, the feeling that the two are incompatible; the people in the audience are at a loss: should they put their faith in the sweetness of the music, or in the strange behavior of the two restrained characters on the stage? Wieland Wagner's Lohengrin is apprehensive from the beginning. One wonders why he came at all. Richard Wagner's Lohengrin, on the other hand, sings: "Elsa, ich liebe dich," and the grandfather's music tells us that his hero is in love. In Bayreuth now we are not permitted to watch the enactment of a romantic story with its musical commentary; we are confronted right away with an interpretation that has lost all belief in the music. The outcome can only be confusion for the novice who sees and hears *Lohengrin* for the first time, and irritation on the part of those who know this work by heart.

Again, only irritation can be the result when we watch the staging of the first scene of Act II of *Lohengrin*. The following is in Wagner's text and score. It is night. Lohengrin and Elsa are celebrating their wedding inside the brightly illuminated castle. Outside, in the dark, are the banished Telramund and his wife Ortrud. Telramund admonishes her to get up so that they can leave together before daybreak. Ortrud, however, does not move; she is cowering on the steps of the cathedral; something is holding her back, some magic force. Telramund sings the line: "Rise, companion of my shame. We must be gone before daybreak." To which Ortrud replies: "I cannot leave. Some spell holds me en-chained." This is followed by Telramund's raging outburst in which he makes her responsible for his present plight. In Wieland Wagner's production the text was intact. But when the curtain went up, Ortrud was standing and Telramund was on the floor. Why should he say to her: "Rise, companion of my shame?" She was standing already, and why should the man singing the role of Telramund be forced to maintain a frozen attitude while utter-ing the most violent *fortissimo* imprecations against Ortrud? Clearly, this did not make sense.

All too often we get the impression that the modern stage director simply wants to spurn tradition. The Bayreuth ending of *The Flying Dutchman* is another case in point. The com-poser's stage directions and his music leave no doubt that the jealous Dutchman sails away toward the end of the opera while Senta, faithful to him, jumps into the sea. Whereupon the red-sailed vessel of the Dutchman sinks, and the hero finds salvation through woman's love. In Wieland Wagner's production the Dutchman died onstage while Senta groped her way through some sort of raised gallery, leaving it to the spectators' imagination whether or not she would jump into the sea. To be sure, Wagner's concluding transfiguration music was cut, for it had lost its mean-ing, but so had the opera called *The Flying Dutchman*.

Throughout this discussion Bayreuth has remained the focal point. In conclusion, however, I should like to widen the radius a bit by indicating that what has happened in Bayreuth during the past decade is symptomatic, to a certain degree, of the stylistic problems that beset other operatic stages in Germany today. Not all of them, to be sure. The Komische Oper in East Berlin, for instance, under the artistic direction of Walter Felsenstein has certainly not fallen under the Bayreuth spell. But Wieland Wag-ner himself carried the torch to Stuttgart; he staged *Tristan* in West Berlin, *Carmen* in Hamburg, and Gluck's *Orfeo* in Munich. Some critics thought that they could discover traces of Bayreuth in a recent production of *Tristan* on the stage of the Vienna Opera. Darmstadt was hardly in need of Wieland Wagner, as the theater there had its Gustav Rudolf Sellner, who has now become the manager of the new Städtische Oper in West Berlin. On the basis of Sellner's record in Darmstadt, it seems likely that the scenic oratorio under his leadership will probably gain momentum in Charlottenburg. At any rate, Sellner invited Wieland Wagner to stage Verdi's *Aïda* in the new opera house, where Wagner succeeded in turning another romantic opera into what one critic described as a "primordial African mysterium," the whole production being bathed in chiaroscuro, to be sure, more *scuro* than *chiaro*.

I am convinced that the impetus for the introduction of static elements into the essentially dynamic form of romantic opera derives from the scenic oratorio—a form which in our century has yielded such outstanding specimens as Stravinsky's *Oedipus Rex,* Milhaud's *Christophe Colomb,* Honegger's *Jeanne d'Arc au bucher,* Carl Orff's *Carmina Burana, Antigonae,* and the *Trionfi,* and Schönberg's *Moses und Aaron.* German designers and directors worked out excellent methods for the staging of these oratorios, and it is my contention that this oratorio style has had a paralyzing influence on the production of essentially dramatic, that is, mimetic opera. The theories behind the "epic theater" of Bert Brecht have likewise leaked into the operatic organism.

There seems to be a confusion here which also prevails in contemporary literary criticism when critics begin to interpret mimetic poetry in terms of didactic allegory. Elder Olson was most outspoken in reaffirming a distinction that was ignored by the so-called New Critics. As he put it so succinctly: "[The plot of a mimetic action] does not, like allegorical action, seek to inculcate certain moral attitudes by arousing our emotions; on the contrary, it makes use of our moral attitudes to arouse our emotions. It does not engage our interest and emotions in particulars of the action in order to instruct us generally; on the contrary, it instructs us about particulars of the characters and actions in the poem in order to engage our emotions and interest in behalf of these very characters and actions." In becoming absorbed in the form of scenic oratorio, a basically didactic and allegorical form, our modern stage directors show a tendency to interpret mimetic poetry and its musical matrix in terms of allegory. There is, to be sure, a dose of allegory and even of doctrine in the works of

Richard Wagner. But this is his most vulnerable aspect which should be underplayed rather than underscored. If Wagner is to remain an emotional experience for generations of opera lovers, the access to him must be left open through the gates of mimetic drama and emotive music.

In our century we have had a Handel renaissance, Gluck revivals, a Mozart cult. Our directors and designers were able to find, in each instance, a style of production which did not do violence to the baroque or rococo spirit of the originals. The Wagner renaissance is still to come. It would entail a return to the composer's conception of romantic opera, a renewed and frank dedication to the genre as such. There should be no need then to be ashamed of the elements of the painted stage or of looking back in anger at Wagner's stage directions. We must disregard *avant-garde* impatience with anything that smacks of theatricality, which is labeled immediately as "phony" by those who most patiently wait for Godot. At any rate, Richard Wagner must not end his dramatic career in the Bauhaus or in some other tomb of allegorical abstraction.

American Drama and the German Stage

WALTHER KARSCH

# American Drama and the German Stage

WALTHER KARSCH

Our theme is the German theater after 1945 and the influence of the American drama on the German stage. What did "German theater" mean in 1945? During the twelve years between 1933 and 1945 many brilliant productions appeared on the German stage. Names such as Jürgen Fehling, Gustaf Gründgens, Heinz Hilpert, Erich Engel, and Hans Schweikart, among others, had kept their distinction, and the bearers of these names attempted not only to rescue the great heritage of the German theater from the time before 1933, but also to develop it further.

The attempt did not succeed, indeed, could not succeed, because in 1933 the German theater was cut off from intellectual and artistic contact with the world and then, during World War II, was isolated from all developments whatsoever. The loss of substance—in both senses of the word—was enormous. First, as far as its knowledge of drama outside Germany was concerned, the German theater in 1945 was suspended in a void; and second, the absolute lack of communication with other stages had caused the theater to freeze stylistically into what, admittedly, was a brilliant rhetorical pose, but also an attitude employing psychological methods that had long since lost their creativity. I do not deny that outstanding performances took place on the municipal and private stages in Berlin, Munich, Düsseldorf, and Hamburg, performances whose high quality is beyond question. During the twelve years of the Third Reich I saw many productions by Fehling, Gründgens, Hilpert, Klöpfer, or Stroux, which, through their sensitive acting and directing, achieved permanent high place in the history of the German theater. But none of this accomplishment was creative or formative in terms of style. Actors and directors could test their merit only in productions left behind by world drama up to Gerhart Hauptmann. Except for a few conversation comedies, the works written for the stage during those twelve years had no dramatic substance. A drying-up process began, at the end of which the German theater found itself entering a void. The arts of acting and directing can develop, of course, even when applied to plays with little poetic merit or literary value. This fact had been proved before in the German theater, during the period, for example, between the death of Hebbel and Hauptmann's first play, *Vor Sonnenaufgang*, when Wildenbruch and Freytag supplied for the German theater plays with no dramatic substance, yet when the theater, thanks primarily to the efforts at Meiningen, evolved a refinement in handicraft and scenic detail that later served well the theater of Brahm and Reinhardt.

After 1945 when the curtain went up again in the old houses or on emergency stages, it seemed that nothing had happened to the German theater. Performances under Karl-Heinz Martin, Hilpert, Gründgens, Fehling, Stroux, Sellner, and Schweikart, among others, were in no way inferior to the performances of former times. Yet something essential had changed. Up to 1933 new talent had constantly been recruited for the theater. Under Brahm, Reinhardt, and Jessner actors had developed who might justly be named in the same breath with the greatest of the German stage. Even between 1933 and 1945 this stream had not completely dried up, although it ran in a narrow bed; it is difficult to add other names besides those of Horst Caspar or Will Quadflieg.

So much for the one side—the art of the theater; now for the other—the art of drama. Brahm's theater and Brahm's style would not have been possible without excellent translations of Ibsen. Reinhardt would not have been possible without Gerhart Hauptmann and Hugo von Hofmannsthal. Fehling, without Barlach, would not have been able to realize his visionary interpretations of dramatists from Shakespeare to Sartre. And without the great Expressionists Jessner would not have become the man who could wring the highest forms of expression from an actor even in front of a bare set.

The situation is the same today—in France, for example, Giraudoux, Claudel, Camus, Sartre, Anouilh, Beckett, Ionesco, Adamov, Audiberti, and Schéhadé have made it possible to find a new style. In England this task fell first to Christopher Fry and T. S. Eliot, then to John Osborne (whose literary merit has also been substantially overrated), and now among others to Brendan Behan and Harold Pinter. For the theater in America this work was performed by Thornton Wilder, Tennessee Williams, Arthur Miller, Edward Albee—without regard for the moment to the differences in their literary quality—among others. Pirandello and the Pirandello renaissance, together with Diego Fabri and Dino Buzzati, prepared the way for the Teatro Piccolo di Milano. In Germany, however, although I could give you the names of numerous authors, only two have had a decisive influence on theater style. One of these, Brecht, died several years ago. The other is young Matthias Braun, whose versions of Aeschylus and Euripides are slowly developing a formative influence on style. Perhaps Leopold Ahlsen might make a third in this small company. After his *Philemon und Baucis,* a piece which operates with old-fashioned naturalistic means but which touches upon poetry, Ahlsen wrote a second play, *Raskolnikoff,* modelled on Dostoevsky but possessed of an individual style giving verbal expression to the intellectual and philosophical situation of man today.

One might object that Dürrenmatt and Frisch should be included with this select group of original and style-forming dramatists, that they have advanced to Broadway, that their plays have made a great stir and have had a formative influence on style, and that it makes no difference that they are Swiss and not German.

That is correct, but Dürrenmatt, apart from *Die Ehe des Herrn Mississippi* and *Der Besuch der alten Damen,* and Frisch, apart from *Die chinesische Mauer,* have not written anything that can be compared with the dramatic work of Hauptmann, of Hofmannsthal, of the Expressionists, of Brecht, or of the very uneven Zuckmayer. To be sure, it is not quantity that matters. But even if we include *Der Graf Öderland* by Frisch and *Romulus der Grosse* by Dürrenmatt, the flow of authentically individual stage language in German—measured by the stream of literature in translation—has not been great enough to imbue German actors and actresses with a new conception of the world through which they could give their audiences new insights into the wealth of world drama.

We must keep in mind, therefore, that our actors, unlike those in America and in other countries, live mainly at secondhand. The great directors such as Gründgens, Kortner, Ludwig Berger, Sellner, Schuh, Stroux, Hans Bauer, Walter Henn, Noelte—all of them, to say nothing of those of second rank—most of the time must play translation-German, sometimes excellent, but on the whole quite miserable. Only in a roundabout way then, through the detour of translation, are the actors able to re-create on the stage the ideas, thoughts, and feelings that compel an author today to give them shape and form.

What I am stressing is the unity between language and style of presentation. Certainly, what Robert Schnorr has re-created out of Christopher Fry and T. S. Eliot, Pinkas Braun out of Edward Albee, and the Tophovens out of Beckett, and what the editors of the Giraudoux edition have done to make up for poor stage translations—this may be poetry and language in the spirit of our times, but still a detour.

Without doubt a whole series of talented actors have grown up during the years following 1945. Of those around forty: Martin Held, Ernst Schroeder, Erich Schellow; of the younger ones: Thomas Holtzmann, Sebastian Fischer; of the women: Gisela Holzinger, Anneliese Roemer, Eva-Katharina Schultz, Christa Keller, Ella Buechi, Hanne Hiob, Heidemarie Theobald, Luitgard Im. Unlike their predecessors, none of them are able to see Shakespeare and Sophocles through the medium of contemporary

German dramatists—only through the roundabout way of the translator.

Such is the situation. One can try to excuse it by saying that German authors were unable to speak after the war because the theaters only repeated the successes of Broadway, West End, and the Champs Elysées. But sixteen years have now elapsed, and in spite of a few new starts nothing has appeared worthy of comparison with the work of Wilder, O'Neill, and Beckett, even that of Anouilh. It is true that our stages after 1945 repeated the plays of foreign authors all too indiscriminately. We stared as though hypnotized at the successes in other countries and did not look too closely at the quality of the authors. Nevertheless, we must not forget that the English, French, and American authors (the Spaniard Lorca and the Italians should be named here too) considered problems which German authors had been prohibited from treating during the period between 1933 and 1945, and forced their audiences into confrontation with them.

High points occurred, such as the first production of Thornton Wilder's *The Skin of Our Teeth* by Stroux, Fehling's brilliantly false interpretation of Sartre's *Les Mouches,* the faithful and yet impressive realization of Miller's *Death of a Salesman* by Käutner with Fritz Kortner, Johanna Hofer, Franz Tillmann, and Berta Drews. Stroux and Kortner interpreted Beckett's *Waiting for Godot* from quite different points of view; Sellner created the style in which Ionesco has to be played in German, as he did for Garcia Lorca and finally for Sartre with *Les Mouches.* Here he found the element of ironic distance, something our directors seldom hit upon, so that dialectical drama of the kind which Sartre and Camus provide in such exemplary fashion is usually, in German, too much burdened with tragic weights. An early postwar example of this heaviness was the brilliant but wrong interpretation of *Les Mouches* by Jürgen Fehling. The handling of Camus' *L'état de siège* by the young director Rudolf Noelte, on the other hand, was a revelation. Henn's world première of Albee's *The Zoo Story* and his interpretation of Beckett's *Krapp's Last Tape* are both achievements of high rank. Boleslav Barlog, director of the Städtische Bühnen in Berlin, must still be mentioned. With the poetic and so undramatic work of Dylan Thomas, *Under*

*Milk Wood,* and recently with his interpretation of Albee's *The American Dream,* Barlog has created a production that is poetic and intellectual, without losing his sense for genuine theater-play. And Gustaf Gründgens, with *The Mansion* by Thomas Wolfe, staged a play that had previously been considered unstageable.

What Willi Schmidt made of Giraudoux's *La Folle de Chaillot,* how he transferred a German author, Franz Kafka, who had not written dramas, to the stage with the help of Max Brod's careful working out of internal and external dialogue in *The Trial,* how then Noelte followed him with *The Castle,* what Hans Lietzau has accomplished through his tenacious wrestling with Ernst Barlach's plays, how Schuh succeeded in presenting the meaning of the dramas of Eugene O'Neill—all of this made us see the world in a completely new light.

These accomplishments are good. Yet if you ask me whether production of mostly foreign plays and the interpretation given them have influenced the style of presentation and the style of German drama, I must answer substantially in the negative. Certainly these great directors have changed the style of presentation by German actors in the last sixteen years—for the better, in fact; but we cannot say, though we should like to say it, that their interpretations of foreign authors or of the works of world literature have had a formative influence on the style of contemporary German drama.

The situation with regard to Bertolt Brecht is completely different. The production of his *Caucasian Chalk Circle* in the translation by John Holmstrom at the new Arena Theater in Washington in 1961 had not the faintest resemblance to the style of the Berlin Ensemble with its deliberate, often violent, alienation effects. Whereas in the Theater am Schiffbauerdamm in East Berlin the players in *The Resistible Rise of Arturo Ui* might exchange roles with each other, the director in Washington merged the actors with their roles in the best world-theater tradition. This style of presentation goes far beyond Brecht; for him the actors were expected to face their roles without inner participation, the performance thereby assuming an instructive and didactic aspect. Gründgens breached Brecht's style radically in the première of *St. Joan of the Stockyards;* Hans Schalla in Bochum and Sellner in Darmstadt also have refused to accept Brecht's theories. Even young Peter Palitsch, Brecht's pupil, who remained in West Germany after the thirteenth of August, failed to follow Brecht, playing *The Trial of Jean d'Arc at Rouen* on the borderline between documentation and poetry.

Whatever your theories, a multitude of problems always emerge. Nothing can be reduced to a common denominator. What, for example, holds for Sellner and his magnificent interpretation of Tennessee Williams' *Camino Real*, probably his best play, does not hold at all for Kortner's interpretation of Miller's travelling salesman. Let us try then on the basis of these two examples to show the varied approaches made to these plays by directors and interpreters.

First, Tennessee Williams. His piece is inconceivable without Hofmannsthal and Claudel, without Brecht and Wilder, without Sartre and Cocteau, without Strindberg and Kafka. And yet it is not a rubbish heap built up from the wastebaskets of world literature. Williams' Kilroy is a creation of his own; he is the American Parzifal, formerly a boxing master with huge fists and small brain, but with a big, good heart that finally is cut from his young body. Sellner did not have Franz Mertz construct, as was done on Broadway, a bright, Mexican-style, operetta square, but rather a dark magic cabinet formed of cloth, upon which the lights, spotlights, and figures of the play were reflected, often glittering and then again cloudy—unusually suggestive, recalling Kafka, gloomy, macabre. Within this frame and against this scenery the actors were deployed in such a way that Sellner, who always proceeds from the dramaturgical-choreographic, could keep his players in a movement that seemed to be pure witchery. Thus Sellner not only set forth Williams' theses and intellectual point of view, but also provided the poetry and the magic without slipping into a lyrical blur. The contours remained firm, despite all the fantasy; the scene served to illuminate the action, as always with Sellner; and whatever Williams had fashioned of symbolism, history, fantasy, and hard reality was analyzed within this frame into its components and combined again into an artistic unity.

Miller's *Death of a Salesman* is quite different, a tragedy of the American travelling salesman, whose dreams far exceed his possibilities and who finally comes to ruin because of the clash between them. That his firm fires him after thirty-four years of activity is ultimately only the occasion of his suicide, not its cause. Under Helmut Käutner's direction Fritz Kortner transformed this tragedy into that of any little man, who might be at home anywhere. This interpretation invalidates the question whether Kortner managed to re-create accurately the American-salesman type. That question is not essential.

What is essential is the human aspect of this tragic situation. Kortner shows us the average human being who ventures to take every hurdle and yet falls even where he encounters no hurdles. Kortner always interprets for us the breach between wish and reality. Within his downtrod man shines the dreamer; within the dreamer shuffles also the downtrod man. Kortner demonstrates much more than realism; he shows the projection of the second self upon the real self. For with Kortner the soul and the intellect are elements of his creative art, and this is far more than realism. A more realistic interpretation of this play was produced under the direction of Erwin Piscator in the Theater am Kurfürstendamm, Berlin, with Steckel as the salesman, Hilde Körber as his wife, and Ronnecker as the son who has failed. Steckel consciously produced the transitions between the downtrod man and the dreamer, depicting a social rather than a human tragedy. That this play has been interpreted realistically is not meaningful except that this production has confirmed the literary value of the piece.

Unfortunately the literary growth of the author has not been confirmed. *The View from the Bridge* is a mixture of Sudermann and of the drama of day-before-yesterday. Miller's gain in theater technique, in external dramaturgy, parallels a loss in poetic substance. *All My Sons* and *Death of a Salesman* had touches of poetic transcendence, a language that was simple, but touching and humanly warm. *The Crucible,* however, already showed violent theater, and ever since its composition Miller has progressed farther toward a concrete, unintellectual, unidimensional theater.

*The Crucible* was given in Berlin and Munich at the same time. Two different directors, of different temperaments (Stroux in Berlin, Schweikart in Munich), made two quite different plays out of the same material. Schweikart reshaped Miller's flatly drawn figures in soft wax; he dampened them wherever possible, let their hard contours blur, and made them more human. Stroux, on the other hand, cut the figures out of hard wood; their contours became even more sharp, and it was clear thereby that whatever is in them is real in the *real* sense, but unreal *poetically*.

Miller takes his stand against any kind of witchhunt, whether it be religious or political. In our Berlin climate this could be successful only if one showed not only the external mechanism of persecution—as Miller does—but also the internal mechanism, and if one laid the motives for it bare. In Berlin we are rather inclined to become impatient when someone makes matters too easy for himself, matters whose gravity we are conscious of, particularly in these times.

In the program notes to *A Memory of Two Mondays,* Miller puts forth a number of shrewd formulations, differentiating between the social drama of our time and that of Ibsen, Shaw, and Chekhov. Yet the "problems" he brings up in this play had already been analyzed much more precisely by Ibsen, criticized much more sarcastically by Shaw, ironized much more delicately by Chekhov, and elevated at last by Strindberg into the universally valid realm of poetry. In the final analysis, this play is just the old familiar milieu-drama trimmed up by Miller with a note of human isolation, a note that has become almost fashionable. Thus without exaggeration and without false national pride we have to say that Arthur Miller has been an original creative artist only in *All My Sons* and in *Death of a Salesman,* and that otherwise he has supplied us only with literature for the theater, competent to be sure, but nothing more than Sudermann adapted to American conditions.

Our verdict on Tennessee Williams does not turn out to be very different. *Camino Real, The Glass Menagerie,* and *A Streetcar Named Desire* have remained his great achievements. What has come since has not fulfilled our hopes. In Tennessee Williams it is not Sudermann, dipped in the American Way of Life, who returns to our stage, but Ibsen and above all Strindberg, not heightened nor deepened by Freud, however, but softened by Freudian banalities, or by a Freud turned into something vulgarly popular through a falsifying, wholly private sexual pathology. One

41

can compare Laura in *The Glass Menagerie* with Blanche in *A Streetcar Named Desire,* and even with Alma in *Summer and Smoke,* since she can still be regarded as a tragic figure; but it is a far way, and unfortunately a downward way, to Serafina in *The Rose Tattoo,* to Brick and Maggie in *Cat on a Hot Tin Roof,* to Alexandra del Lago and Wayne in *Sweet Bird of Youth,* and finally to Sebastian Vanabel in *Suddenly Last Summer,* whose horrible fate is only told—not seen on the stage. The way leads down from the heights of *Camino Real* into the abysses of a primitive pathology and is of lesser interest.

Yet Williams and Miller, whose magnificent stage technique might have had a fruitful effect on the German theater, once were among our favorites. That their influence has dwindled to practically nothing lies in the fact that over the course of the years poetic substance in both authors has diminished.

What is the situation with regard to authors who are of far less significance than Miller or Williams? After the war a veritable invasion of American authors mounted our stages. In the rear guard of this invasion are many authors who from the start were not bent on supplying dramatic literature of poetic or literary value: Inge, Patrick, van Druten, Lillian Hellman, Behrman. We learned much about the American Way of Life from their works, for example, from van Druten's *I Remember Mama.* Zuckmayer, who translated the play for the German stage, wrote:

What induced me to make this play available to the German-speaking public is its human content, that is, the presentation of a section of everyday American life that is little known in Europe, but which is more characteristic and significant of the real America than all those things generally taken to be American.

Van Druten has helped us considerably to understand what America and its inhabitants claim to be, as has Inge, in *The Dark at the Top of the Stairs, Bus Stop, Picnic,* and *Come Back Little Sheba,* plays in which the life of the American small town is affectionately depicted. With his delineation of emotional futility in an unfulfilled marriage in *Come Back Little Sheba,* the presentation of frustrated mediocrity in terms of a tragic figure, Inge's art of characterization has undoubtedly enriched the German stage, forcing directors and actors into more subtle presentations. Thornton Wilder must be mentioned as one of this group. We Germans completely misunderstood him at first, principally because we took him much too seriously, because we overlooked the ironical detachment with which he treats his figures. But of this later.

I want now to turn to those plays in which America discusses its political problems, often in a form that has significance beyond America, for example, Lillian Hellman's *On the Other Side*. Miss Hellman, I believe, destroyed the effect of her play because her Count is not really a political opponent of the engineer Mueller, but rather an ordinary swindler from the Balkans. Hence the dialectical tension diminishes very quickly, the play soon slips down to a level on which it is easy to decide in favor of the good.

Similarly, an uncomfortable feeling steals over the thoughtful German spectator when he sees plays like Robert Penn Warren's *The Governor,* Gore Vidal's *The Best Man,* or Saul Levitt's *Andersonville Trial*. In all three the author's sympathies are so much on the side of one figure, that genuine curiosity, suspense, and interest can hardly arise.

And now we come at the end, as always, to the poets, to Thomas Wolfe, Thornton Wilder, Elmer Rice, Archibald MacLeish, William Faulkner, Edward Albee, Ezra Pound, and above all Eugene O'Neill. Pardon me please if I become a little rhetorical and tell you that we should thank the muses on our knees that you have these authors. Of course, Elmer Rice's *Dream Girl* does not have the qualities of *The Adding Machine,* and even Wilder and O'Neill have written mediocre plays. Nevertheless, one feels in *Dream Girl* Rice's power of psychological penetration, tempered here with irony, kindly superiority, genuine wit, and heart, without its becoming *gemütlich*. Mister Zero in *The Adding Machine* is more malicious. This is one of those plays which are intellectually and emotionally naked, which are far from any kind of naturalism or realism and display only the scaffolds of emotional and intellectual construction, divested not only of all ornament but also of all flesh. For all its accusation against society, Rice's play is also a drama of accusation against the individual who willingly lets his individuality be buried, feels at home in mechanized life and does not rebel, as he would be justified in doing, for the purpose of redeeming himself from his state of emotional and intellectual torpidity.

Another theater poet is William Saroyan. In Berlin we have seen his *My Heart's in the Highlands, The Time of Your Life,* and *Paris Comedy.* These are not theater pieces in the proper sense, but musical variations on a theme, and that is how they were played in our country. That a poet, as in *My Heart's in the Highlands,* prefers to suffer hunger and allows himself to be evicted in a kindly, amiable fashion, instead of holding a sensible job, that he encourages his son to steal fruit or beg from a shopkeeper, that an old actor flees from the old people's home, entices alms from his good neighbors with the simple tunes of his horn, and dies in the poet's hut while playing the role of the dying Lear—all this is scarcely action. With Saroyan everything remains music.

Unfortunately, one of your great writers of fiction wrote only one piece for the theater, *The Mansion,* and to the honor of the German stage I must say that this drama received its world première in Germany. Not much takes place in this play by Thomas Wolfe, nor does the dialogue have much dramatic force, but it is a fine poetical work for the theater. In the prologue Wolfe displays the whole force of a white conqueror, in the first scene the assurance of one who has risen from conqueror to master. But then the dramatic structure begins to crumble.

Another piece for the theater was extracted by the dexterous Ketti Frings from the great novel *Look Homeward Angel,* but little was left of one of the most splendid narrative works of literature.

And what is the situation with respect to Ezra Pound? The most likely German author to be compared with him would be Matthias Braun, who has also attempted to cast ancient drama into modern form. Pound did this with Sophocles' *The Women of Trachis,* but it is hard to decide whether this is a new translation, a free rendering, or a reshaping of the Sophoclean subject.

Archibald MacLeish in his *J. B.* certainly does not have Pound's strong power of language and thought. This modern variant of the Job theme is a radical denial of man's, even the most pious man's, claim to grace. This rich Mr. Job, for whom everything works out well—business, wife, and five children—loses everything in the end. At the conclusion he has leprosy and suffers senseless blows of fate, about which his wife Sarah remonstrates with him and with God. Yet at the conclusion the two begin all over again. Unfortunately, this conclusion does not seem to be quite conclusive, for in the last critical scenes the arguments with which Job and God affirm their separate existences are diluted into aphorisms.

Here Wilder is more human, if you will. *The Skin of Our Teeth* might perhaps be entitled "It's Always the Same Thing Over Again." The Man, a commonplace person with ambitions, at the same time obsessed by a sense of intellectual responsibility, is caught between the watchfulness of a true woman and the dangerousness of one who—in housemaid's dress, in the daring costume of a beauty queen, or in the uniform of an army nurse— always represents the temptation to break out of the usual and accustomed. Rejected time and again at the critical moment, she does not disappear, however, because she belongs to life and to men. She is always taken along and has her place beside the eternally burning fire in the congealing glacial world round about, in the Ark of Noah, and in peacetime.

It is not my task to resketch this play here, for it is familiar to all. It was much played in our country after the war, often too heavily, but now I think the German stage has finally found the right style. It helped us very much after the war, for in spite of the frightful things that take place, it is not a pessimistic play. It presents life as it is, and advises that one accept it, put up with it, take hold of it. Walls are crushed by glaciers, are knocked down by the air-pressure of bombs; the earth drowns in water. Those who are saved are always the same ones who were shipwrecked, and their needs are always the same: bread and books, the body and the spirit; wife and mistress, Eros and sex; procreation and murder, Hymen and Cain.

Wilder's other pieces do not have the strength of *The Skin of Our Teeth*, not even *Our Town*—although its insight into the world of Americans was of great interest to us. Nevertheless, we envy you Americans for the force of mind, language, and form that speaks even from Wilder's lesser works and which is evident even when he makes *The Matchmaker* out of Nestroy's *Einen Jux will er sich machen.*

Two narrative writers who have also written plays might still be named: John Steinbeck with his marvellously lyrical human drama, *Of Mice and Men;* and the great confession of guilt on the part of Temple Stevens, née Drake, which William Faulkner has sifted out in his *Requiem for a Nun.*

Then finally there is the great O'Neill. When I say that he, too, issues from Strindberg, that Kafka was surely not unknown to him, that he has drawn his knowledge of the human soul from C. G. Jung, that he is a master of the dramatic techniques of Ibsen and Hauptmann and even, at times, of Sudermann—I do not mean this as a reproach. *The Iceman Cometh, Anna Christie, The Hairy Ape, A Touch of the Poet, Mourning Becomes Electra, Long Day's Journey into Night, Hughie, A Moon for the Misbegotten*—what would the theater be without these plays? O'Neill's work has, without becoming in the least archaic, taken on the stature of antiquity. What realism, naturalism, psychologism have taken to pieces, O'Neill—in this respect, and not only in this respect, an inherently creative descendant of Strindberg—has put back together. His figures have become exemplary once more.

We are at the end and yet not at the end. O'Neill was born in 1888 and died in 1953 at the age of sixty-five. Edward Albee, probably the youngest current American dramatist, was born in 1928. The world première of *The Zoo Story* took place in Berlin in 1959. Since then we have seen *The Death of Bessie Smith* and *The American Dream. The Death of Bessie Smith* is dramatics of the day before yesterday, exactly as in Miller's case, dear old milieu-dramatics, which Albee tries to make palatable for us with sexual explication. In *The American Dream* Albee imitates Ionesco, and however spendidly the figures talk at cross-purposes, Ionesco has done better in *La Cantatrice Chauve.* In the Berlin performance, under Thomas Holtzmann's intelligent analysis of the text and his impressively intensified rendering, *The Zoo Story* took on a power that moved deeply, carried one away, and at the end called forth vigorous applause.

Closing with this analysis of a world première may give a glance into the theatrical workshop that is the German stage, and may provide Americans with new insights into their drama.

Thespian Austria

WILHELM SCHLAG

# Thespian Austria

## WILHELM SCHLAG

When people speak of Austrian theater they usually think of the Burgtheater, perhaps also of the Theater in der Josefstadt, and if they are musically inclined, of the Staatsoper. The summer tourist with cultural interests, who has foresightedly reserved his tickets well in advance, will also rave about the Salzburg Festival.

Yet Austria offers more than highly sophisticated forms of dramatic art. At Christmas time, for example, on the night of December 5, many villages throughout the country will be visited by the bearded St. Nikolaus. The plays celebrating his appearance are intended to expound Christian tenets, but the goodly saint is also accompanied by sinister companions, a symbolic reminder out of the dim pagan past that winter brings the forces of darkness and that these are hostile to the good spirits which make the grass sprout in the fields, the cattle and the sheep bear young. Magic might help, and so, during the long nights of late fall and early winter, mummers personifying fertility and its antagonists once roamed through the villages and towns. Even today in Mitterndorf in Styria, for example, the old struggle between light and darkness, life and death, good and evil, breaks out anew every spring. Winter retreats only slowly and grudgingly in the mountains and deep valleys, and one needs to help it along.

These vestiges of magic are, of course, only a tradition nowadays or an occasion for simple merrymaking. But such celebrations allow the rural folk to indulge their love for spectacle and to display their creative talent in the making of masks and colorful costumes. Most of these pageants require a great deal of improvisation, but the Christmas and Passion plays call also for conscientious study of roles and characters. In the Tyrol alone more than a hundred groups of folk players now perform on peasant stages. The best-known Passion plays are those at Erl and Thiersee in the Tyrol, and at Kirchschlag in Lower Austria. As a genre, the religious play has also been adopted into modern drama, most notably by Hugo von Hofmannsthal, who created new versions of *Everyman* and of Calderón's *Gran teatro del mundo,* and by Max Mell, with his *Nachfolge Christi-Spiel, Apostelspiel,* and *Schutzengelspiel.*

I shall speak later about the survival, or revival, of the folk stage in Vienna. Here I should like to mention another old form of the theater that is still holding its own in Austria, the puppet play. As *Kasperltheater* it is as much a delight to children now as it was for Goethe over two hundred years ago. Kasperl is the "funny guy [*lustige Person*]," a direct descendant of Hanswurst and Staberl. In the early days puppet players travelled from town to town, from church fair to church fair. The first permanent puppet theater on German-speaking territory was founded in the Judenhof in Vienna in 1667. *Dr. Faustus* was performed there, with accompanying melodies and ballet. Joseph Haydn wrote five operettas for Prinz Esterhazy's puppet theater in Eisenstadt. As a form of art the puppet play was perfected in Vienna by Professor Richard Teschner, whose little theater is preserved in the theater collection of the Austrian National Library. Here, from time to time, his widow and former assistants put on a performance. The *Marionettentheater* of Professor Aichner in Salzburg, which was on tour in the United States a few years ago, is also renowned. I shall have some-

thing to say later about the role of this art form in educating young
people for the theater.

The roots of the modern Austrian theater are, of course, neither
pagan rites nor the puppet theater, but the courtly play, which is
far removed from the rollicking improvisations of the earthy Hanswurst. We can trace these roots far back into the Middle Ages.
While the Alsatian Reinmar von Hagenau, the Tyrolian Walther
von der Vogelweide, and other Minnesingers were entertaining
Leopold V and his retinue in Vienna, the populace watched the
religious plays in the market squares or churches of the city. They
were moved by the poverty of Mary and Joseph and the stable at
Bethlehem, they rejoiced at the antics of a clowning shepherd, and
they laughed when St. Peter drew his sword and smote off Malchus'
ear.

At the end of the Middle Ages the Habsburg Emperor Maximilian I, a Renaissance *uomo universale,* last knight and humanist,
brought Conrad Celtis, Johannes Stabius, Johann Cuspinian, and
other German humanists, to Vienna. At the University of Vienna,
Celtis revived the comedies of Plautus and Terence and the dramas
of Seneca. He himself wrote a *Ludus Dianae* and a rhapsodic play
glorifying Maximilian's deeds. For the double wedding of the
Emperor's grandchildren, Ferdinand and Maria, in 1515, Benedic-
tus Chelidonius, abbot of the *Schottenkloster,* wrote and produced
(with the aristocratic students of the monastery) *Voluptatis cum
virtute disceptatio,* an allegoric paraphrase of the classical Greek
theme concerning the choice of Hercules. These plays, combining
poetry with choral music, are predecessors of the baroque *Ludi
Caesari* later produced by the Jesuits, who adopted the school
drama as one means to further the Counter-Reformation. They
took topics from the Old and New Testaments and adapted themes
from Greek mythology. Orestes pursued by the Erinyes, for instance, was intended to signify the guilty conscience. Thus the
Jesuit drama acquired its characteristic dichotomous form as a
play *and* an allegorical interpretation. The greatest of the Viennese
Jesuit dramatists, Nicolaus Avancini, made liberal use of classic
mythology in glorifying the Catholic Church and the Habsburg
dynasty. His works often combined poetry with music, dance and

pageantry. Edifying religious and historical genre-pictures relating to the House of Austria were also popular—and long-winded. In 1608 the story of St. Leopold, the Babenberg patron saint of Austria, was unfolded in 106 major parts. In 1611 the performance of *St. Matthias in Scharka* lasted two days. It was accompanied by a "Necessary Instruction for the Better Understanding of the Story," so that the audience would become better acquainted with certain aspects of the history of Bohemia. The play ended with an apotheosis of the future Habsburg king of Bohemia, Matthias.

Although the Jesuit theater was sponsored by the Court, it was popular with the rank and file. Crowds were so large that the dialogue was sometimes drowned out by the noise from the audience. Emperor Leopold I, himself no mean composer and musician, seldom missed a performance. In 1665, when the producers apologized to him for a performance that had lasted six hours, he indicated that it had continued, on the contrary, too short a time. His love for the theater withstood even tragedy. In 1662, after an overcrowded grandstand collapsed during an open-air presentation at the Court, he wrote to a *confidant*: "This pre-Lenten season should have been rather quiet on account of the mourning, but we had a few small festivities behind closed doors; after all, it doesn't help the dead to be sad."

But Leopold's greatest love was the opera, which at that time was Italian. At his wedding to the Infanta Margareta Teresa of Spain in December, 1666, the *dramma per musica, Il pomo d'oro,* was performed with a cast of over a thousand. The festivities, which lasted several weeks, opened with an equestrian ballet. In the first part, an allegorical contest of the elements, the Emperor himself acted.

Italian influence made itself felt not only on the music and theater at court, but also, through the *commedia dell'arte,* on the outdoor productions for the common people, which, set up on crude platforms, provided the Viennese with a rough, sometimes rather low type of comedy. In 1670, arguing the new-fangled mercantilist thesis that money should not leave the country—as it would if foreign companies were received—the Imperial Court Clerk Peter Mueller begged for an imperial patent to form his own company in order to replace the travelling groups presenting this type of play. He promised to "prove there was nothing the Italians can

do which the Germans could not do just as well." Judged by contemporary reports, however, extemporaneous comedy in German
was of extremely low caliber in Vienna until the beginning of the
eighteenth century, when the Styrian actor and dentist Josef Anton
Stranitzky re-created Hanswurst. This venerable medieval figure,
returning in the guise of an itinerant *Kraut und Sauschneider*
from Salzburg, at once became the darling of the Viennese.
Stranitzky and his successors ridiculed the anachronisms and
pompous monstrosities of baroque absolutism and poked fun at
public figures, frequently at the risk of offending the authorities.
And since theirs was not a prudish audience, Hanswurst's jests and
slapstick were often decidedly risqué.

On December 14, 1716, in a letter from Vienna to England,
Lady Mary Wortley Montagu reported her impressions of such a
performance in occasionally shocked tones.

But if their operas are thus delightful, their comedies are in as high
a degree ridiculous. They have but one playhouse, where I had the
curiosity to go to a German comedy, and was very glad it happened to
be the story of Amphitrion, that subject already having been handled
by a Latin, French, and English poet, I was curious to see what an
Austrian author would make of it. I understand enough of the language to comprehend the greatest part of it; and besides, I took with
me a lady, who had the goodness to explain to me every word. The
way is, to take a box, which holds four, for yourself and company.
The fixed price is a gold ducat. I thought the house very low and dark;
but I confess the comedy admirably recompensed that defect. I never
laughed so much in my life. It began with Jupiter's falling in love out
of a peep-hole in the clouds, and ended with the birth of Hercules. But
what was most pleasant, was the use Jupiter made of his metamorpho-
sis; for you no sooner saw him under the figure of Amphitrion, but,
instead of flying to Alcmena with the raptures Mr. Dryden puts into
his mouth, he sends for Amphitrion's tailor and cheats him of a lace
coat, and his banker of a bag of money, a Jew of a diamond ring, and
bespeaks a great supper in his name; and the greatest part of the comedy
turns upon poor Amphitrion's being tormented by these people for
their debts, and Mercury uses Sosias in the same manner. But I could
not easily pardon the liberty the poet has taken of larding his play with
not only indecent expressions, but such gross words as I don't think our
mob would suffer from a mountebank; and the two Sosiases very fairly

let down their breeches in the direct view of the boxes, which were full of people of the first rank, that seemed very well pleased with their entertainment, and they assured me that this was a celebrated piece.

Lady Montagu was not the only one who had reservations about Hanswurst. When circles close to the Court, and then the Court itself, began to be interested in him and his merry companions, the actors were forced to display more decorum. In 1751, when a theatrical censorship was decreed imposing severe restrictions on extemporizing, the very life of Hanswurst and his ilk was threatened. Furthermore, German literature was on the rise, and the opposition to Italian and French influences mounting. In 1770 the famous Joseph von Sonnenfels, who had been waging a running battle with the popular Hanswurst, made a passionate appeal to Emperor Joseph II for the foundation of a German national theater which should be free, not only of foreign influences, but also of burlesque. The request was granted. In 1776 the Burgtheater was founded. At the beginning a court theater, this institution later became a theater for the *haute bourgeoisie*, and after opening the doors to Ferdinand Raimund and Johann Nestroy, thus amalgamating the courtly and the popular elements of the Austrian theater, became a theater of the people. During the last days of World War II, after having been closed for ten months, the great theater building on the Ring went up in flames. The task of reconstruction was staggering. One-fifth of the city had been destroyed; there were severe shortages of goods and materials; and the Staatsoper, which had also been destroyed, had priority. In 1955, however, only a few weeks after the Opera had been reopened with *Fidelio,* the new-old Burg was dedicated with a performance of Franz Grillparzer's *König Ottokars Glück und Ende.*

For ten long years, then, from the end of World War II to the reopening of the building on the Ring, the Burgtheater was housed in the Ronacher, once known as the home of sophisticated vaudeville. It was hardly suitable for theater in the grand manner. During the first years after the war not only fuel was lacking, but also textiles for costumes, paint for the scenery, and even paper on which to print the programs. There were frequent power failures. Amidst all these difficulties the Burgtheater demonstrated that it was not a building but an ensemble and an idea. It had remained faithful to the purpose stated so succinctly by its great director, Heinrich Laube:

My ideal was to be able to say after a few years to every guest from abroad—stay a year in Vienna and attend the Burgtheater; you'll see all the classics that German literature has created for the stage in the last century. You'll also see what Shakespeare has left us Germans and everything created in Romance Languages that can be adapted to our way of thinking and feeling.

Laube's ideal was reaffirmed at the opening of the reconstructed house by Friedrich Schreyvogl, assistant director of the Burg-theater and a descendant of the great Joseph Schreyvogel, who gave the theater its permanent form during the long years of his directorship (1814–1832). The Burgtheater, Schreyvogl wrote, should again be "a world theater, a forum for intellectual exchange covering American and European, as well as Austrian and German, theater life."

The repertory of the Burgtheater implements this concept, with plays presented on two stages, the house on the Ringstrasse and the Akademietheater. Equal attention is given to classics, problem plays, sophisticated modern comedies, and the delightful folk plays of Raimund and Nestroy, interlarded with music and satire. From the ancient Greek dramatists to Shakespeare, from Calderón, Lope de Vega, Racine, Molière, Ibsen, Strindberg, and Chekhov to the modern American, English, and French playwrights, the world's great dramatists are all presented. In the coming Shakespeare Year (1964) the old custom of presenting play series will be revived with the production of Shakespeare's historical dramas.

As a rule, the Burgtheater performs plays that have been tested by time and on other stages. It has, however—and not surprisingly for Austria's foremost stage—also presented the world premières of many plays by Austrian authors (Czokor, Mell, Hochwälder, Zusanek, Billinger, and others), as well as numerous first produc-tions in German. In every case the Burgtheater has observed four tenets: that it should present world theater; that it can and must do so with the free exchange of ideas; that it is a theater for the people; and that its public expects a *Schauspielkunst in Vollen-dung*, that is, perfection in the art of acting.

The postwar development of the Josefstädtertheater, or Theater in the Josefstadt, Vienna's most important private stage, is an effect of changes within the structure of the class that has always supported it. As part of Hitler's Germany, Austria before 1945 had been politically and intellectually shut off for seven years from those countries which did not side with the Axis. The Nazi suppression of free thought, together with military exigencies, was not exactly conducive to a flowering of the arts, and in 1944 the theaters closed completely in Germany—*silent musae inter arma*. After the war people with cultural aspirations felt a tremendous need to catch up, to replace what they had lost. Material goods were scarce; theater and movie tickets were among the best bargains. At the theater one could forget the drabness and misery of the world outside.

After the drastic currency reform of 1948, and through priming by the Marshall Plan, the economy began to recover. With this improvement another and even more urgent demand could be satisfied—the need for consumer goods. The cultured middle class, which had made up the bulk of theatergoers in Austria, had, and still has, relatively the lowest income. Its members were forced to spend their money on necessities. On the other hand the *nouveaux riches,* who have invariably appeared in the wake of destruction since ancient times and who again emerged during the *Wirtschaftswunder* of the 1950's, wanted entertainment but no problems. This conflict of interests resulted in a theater crisis that could be overcome only by good management, by careful selection of the repertory, and—*ultima ratio* in the modern welfare state—by governmental subsidies. It is interesting to see how the Theater in der Josefstadt met this situation. It closed its second boulevard theater, the Bürgertheater, which had been intended to help satisfy the craving for entertainment during the theater boom after the war; and it assigned the sparkling, sometimes slightly frivolous, but intensely entertaining conversation piece which the Viennese love so dearly to the Josefstädtertheater's Kammerspiele in the First District. This is now Vienna's leading boulevard theater. The old house in the Eighth District, that is, in the Josefstadt, produces so-called world theater or, as Otto Basil, the eminent Viennese critic, called it, boulevard theater with a claim to distinction. In 1957 the Josefstädtertheater also took over the Kleines Theater im Konzerthaus, which it runs as an experimental stage.

The off-Broadway type of theater has become an important feature of Vienna's theatrical life. A large theater cannot experiment without risking financial loss or decreased prestige. The very *raison d'etre* of the small stage, however, is precisely such experimentation. Foremost amongst these theaters in Vienna is the Theater der Courage, directed by Stella Cadmon. It was preceded by some interesting experimentation. In 1931 Miss Cadmon had founded a cabaret, Der liebe Augustin, in the basement of the Cafe Prückel. The owner had told her, "I shall give you the basement free if your audience orders at least thirty cups of coffee per performance." In this way, as Miss Cadmon stated on mimeographed announcements for the first performance, she and a few colleagues, fellow students from the Vienna Academy of Music and Dramatic Art, began to offer her audience "Jazz and *Butterkipferln, Guglhupf* and Satire, Sandwiches and *Romantik*, Beer and *neue Sachlichkeit*, Sausages and Soul." Like most of the stages following Stella Cadmon's example—Die Literatur am Naschmarkt, Kabarett ABC, and Stachelbeere—Der liebe Augustin came to an end in March, 1938. In 1945 Miss Cadmon reopened her cabaret and in 1950 she converted it into the Theater der Courage, opening with Bertolt Brecht's *Furcht und Elend des Dritten Reiches*. The name of the theater was aptly chosen. In twelve years Stella Cadmon has produced ninety different plays. Twenty of these productions were world premières or first performances in German, and at least one of them, the world première of *Das Schweigen* by the Polish dramatist Roman Brandstätter, caused an international sensation.

The Studio junger Schauspieler, later known as Theater der 49—the number representing the fact that a theater seating less than fifty persons requires no license—has produced plays mostly by Austrian dramatists. The most professional of the basement or *Kellertheater* was the Theater am Parkring, which opened in 1949 with plays by Lope de Vega and Büchner, and closed in 1959. The year 1949 also witnessed the founding of Das Experiment, which was renamed the Kleines Theater im Konzerthaus when Michael Kehlmann joined it as artistic director in 1950. Helmut Qualtinger, Luise Martini, Gerhard Bronner, and Carl Merz soon joined the new stage, and the result of this pooling of talent was an immensely popular satirical theater, typically represented by such works as *Reigen 51* and *Brettl vor dem Kopf*. Many of the songs produced by this foursome have become classics, for example, the take-off on Marlon Brando's "The Wild One," *der Wilde* in this case being a Viennese *blouson noir,* proud owner of a motor-bike, who makes such statements as "I don't know where I'm going, but I'm bound to get there faster [*I was zwoa net woar i hifoa, dafia bin i g'schwinda duat*]."

Since the Kleines Theater im Konzerthaus was taken over by the Theater in der Josefstadt, in 1957, it has presented here, on its third stage, those modern and avant-gardist plays whose performance in the house in the Eighth District appears too great a financial risk. Qualtinger, Bronner, Merz, and Martini left to open their own house, the Theater am Kärntnertor, and continued to offer nightly proof that Vienna's wit and humor, which kindled Stranitzky and Nestroy, are still very much alive. Here, on the same spot where Stranitzky leased his theater from the city in 1710, the indomitable Qualtinger and his congenial friends levelled their guns at conceit and incompetence, at officialdom and the man-in-the-street, at the *jeunesse dorée* and juvenile delinquents, at their compatriots and other inhabitants of this globe, and at the false gods of our time.

In the suburbs other small stages came into being. They include Das Atelier, successor to Das Kaleidoskop, and Das Experiment, both of which play surrealist theater. The Theater der Tribüne specializes in first performances of Austrian authors. The Studio der Hochschulen belongs in a category of its own. During the first hectic postwar years the Studio attracted students of Thespian ambition who had gone through the holocaust of World War II. Most of these had witnessed the total collapse of the Third Reich and were merely existing in an ideological vacuum, intellectually starved. They tackled everything. To one shocked Viennese critic, reviewing a performance of Büchner's *Woyzeck,* "The actors were in a state of intoxication and put their audience in a similar state.

This is the beginning and the end of all art." Many actors, stage designers, and directors received their theatrical baptism in this Studio. By the time the fire had died down, in 1955, the Studio had to its credit some sixty-five productions, including thirteen world premières or first performances, and several guest performances in other European countries.

The Austrian effort to bring theater to the people may be illustrated by brief descriptions of one other stage in Vienna and of two in the provinces.

Toward the end of the last century the Burgtheater had lost its aristocratic and court connections and had become a theater for the middle classes, primarily for the *haute bourgeoisie*. In order that the theater might be accessible also to the craftsmen in the suburbs, the emerging white-collar workers, the teachers, and the civil servants in the lower echelons, the Volkstheater was founded in 1889. To this day it has remained faithful to that purpose. Approximately 22,000 subscribers are given tickets at reduced prices for eleven performances. (I might mention in this connection that, while salaries and wages have been increased tenfold since 1937, the price of theater tickets has merely tripled.) Subscription performances sell almost 75 percent of the seats in advance; 10 percent more are sold to the general public; thus 85 percent of house capacity is filled for at least four hundred performances per year, adding up to approximately 510,000 theater visitors. In the average year thirteen first performances are given, and since 1955 guest performances in the suburbs also have been made in suitable moviehouses, school auditoriums, and similar buildings. During the season 1960–1961 an experiment entitled "Theater without Compromise" (*Kompromissloses Theater*) was initiated in order to offer three avant-gardist plays per year under the subscription plan. Fifty-five percent of the cost for operation of the Volkstheater is covered by the sale of tickets, the remainder by state subsidy.

In Vorarlberg, Austria's westernmost state, none of the towns are large enough to support a permanent local stage. A travelling Theater für Vorarlberg has remedied this situation. It is a private theater which has been granted a license by the state on the condition that it give at least twenty performances a month and at least nine new productions each season. The expenses for the current season have been estimated at two million Austrian shillings. Fifty-nine percent of this cost is covered by subsidy, which includes contributions from the state of Vorarlberg, the Austrian Federal Ministry of Education, and the towns and communities of Vorarlberg. The headquarters of this travelling stage is in Bregenz.

In Burgenland, Austria's easternmost province, the situation is similar to that in Vorarlberg. The Burgenländische Landesbühne is also a travelling theater, playing on the average to audiences in twenty-five different localities throughout the province each year. It devotes much of its time to introducing Märchen-plays, as well as the classics, to school children.

As further evidence for the democratization of the Austrian theater, it should be mentioned that all large Austrian theaters offer subscriptions, and that the Austrian trade unions sometimes buy up all tickets for a scheduled performance and sell them at reduced prices to interested members.

The lofty edifice of the theater must have a firm and large base. In Austria the Theater der Jugend is probably the most interesting means so far employed to ensure such a base. Originally conceived in 1932 by educators and persons actively engaged in theatrical work who were concentrating their efforts on the so-called *Mittelschulen* that prepare students for the university, the Theater der Jugend went into eclipse during World War II, but was revived in 1945. For some young people in the first postwar years the theater was merely an escape, but for most it carried a message in a very troubled time. It gave them ideals and, above all, made them enthusiastic and knowledgeable theatergoers. Today, even more than ten or fifteen years ago, it is important to arouse the interest of young people and to give them opportunity to visit the theater, the opera, and the concert hall, for a century grown prosperous offers all too many distractions, some of which require no personal engagement or commitment. Through a periodical, *Neue Wege,* the Theater der Jugend offers an outlet for various forms of artistic expression and a forum for promising young artists.

The ground for such dramatic experience is prepared step by

step. First, there is the puppet show, with its visits to the schools; next come plays for children. Since the legitimate theater offers little in this field, the Theater der Jugend stages its own productions in Vienna's Renaissance-bühne. At fourteen years of age, following a carefully selected program, the children begin to attend the regular theaters. The most mature group subscribes to a project called "World Theater and Experiment." A subscription comprises eight to ten performances. Tickets at reduced prices are also made available, of course, outside of, and in addition to, regular subscriptions.

During the season of 1959–1960, 774,397 participants in the Theater der Jugend attended a total of 1,698 performances. Attendants at 646 performances of the federal and private theaters and of the experimental stages numbered 527,040; 138,323 went to 136 concerts also sponsored by the Theater der Jugend; 50,373 attended 281 lectures or guided tours. Members of the Theater der Jugend also attended 55,719,605 performances of puppet plays.

Not the least of the means for educating a public eager for the theater is the sale of standing room. Its low cost makes the theater accessible even to the poorest student—that is, if he has the stamina to stand hours in line for a première or other important event. As the initiated know, it is "the fourth gallery" which often decides the mood of an audience.

The training of new actors is chiefly entrusted to the Reinhardt Seminar, a department of the Academy of Music and Dramatic Art in Vienna. It has at its disposal the magnificent Schlosstheater in Schönbrunn. Future directors and dramaturgists attend the Theaterwissenschaftliches Institut at the University of Vienna. The Mozarteum in Salzburg also has a drama department. The academies in Vienna and Salzburg and the Conservatory of the City of Vienna likewise offer courses in opera and ballet. Stage design is taught at the Reinhardt Seminar of the Academy of Fine Arts in Vienna, as well as at the Academy of Applied Arts. Many of the graduates of these institutions gain their first practical experience on the experimental little stages.

The best-known Austrian festivals are probably those in Salzburg. But the idea of a *Festspiel* there is older than Max Reinhardt and Hugo von Hofmannsthal. What was probably the first opera performance in a German-speaking country—an open-air performance, by the way—took place under Archbishop Markus Sittikus von Hohenems in the Steintheater of Hellbrunn in 1617 and 1618. In 1842 the first Mozart celebration was held in connection with the unveiling of a monument to the great musician. In 1887 Hans Richter suggested that such celebrations become a regular feature of Salzburg life and that a Festspielhaus be built. In 1916 a Committee for the Salzburg Festival House was constituted. When Gerhart Hauptmann learned of this event he wrote:

Mozart celebrations and a Mozart Festival House in Salzburg—that is the most natural and most fortunate of ideas. An ever-bubbling spring of purest poetry in the middle of a marvelous city and a magnificent landscape. Wouldn't everyone like to make a pilgrimage there, with men of peace, out of the darkness of this ravaged age?

The Board of Directors of the Festival Community was assisted by an advisory committee on art, composed of Max Reinhardt, Franz Schalk, and Richard Strauss. Hugo von Hofmannsthal and Alfred Roller were soon asked to participate. On August 15, 1918, the first general assembly of the Festival Community took place in Mirabell Palace. Various schemes and locations for a Festspielhaus were considered. The choice finally fell on Hellbrunn for the site and on the architectural plans by Professor Hans Poelzig. Ground was broken in 1922. In the meantime, in August, 1920, the first performance of Hofmannsthal's *Jedermann* had taken place. It is no coincidence that Hofmannsthal, after the apocalyptic war and during the chaotic period which followed it, chose to make the old morality play, *Das Spiel vom Leben und Sterben des reichen Mannes,* the central theme of the festival. The first operas —by Mozart, of course—were performed in 1922.

The high degree of inflation after the end of World War I prevented the execution of Poelzig's plans. As a substitute, the Winterreitschule in the Hofmarstall building was remodelled and opened in 1925 with Hofmannsthal's *Salzburger grosses Welttheater,* Max Mell's *Apostelspiel,* and Karl Vollmoeller's *Mirakel.* In the Stadttheater *Don Juan* was performed under Karl Muck, *Figaros Hochzeit* under Franz Schalk, and *Don Pasquale* under

Bruno Walter. In 1926 Clemens Holzmeister, Austria's foremost architect, remodelled the Festspielhaus, creating room for twelve hundred people. In 1937, at Toscanini's suggestion, Holzmeister again remodelled the building, this time radically. Finally, in 1956, ground was broken for an entirely new Festspielhaus, again according to plans by Clemens Holzmeister. The new house was opened in 1960 with Richard Strauss's *Der Rosenkavalier* and Frank Martin's *Mysterium von der Geburt des Herrn*.

Although the Salzburg Festivals were originally designed for stage plays, they have included opera more and more frequently. When the festivals were resumed in 1945 Ernst Lothar recalled the earlier purpose by producing a *Jedermann* which was intended not merely to continue a tradition but to have meaning for a generation that had gone through a genocidal war. Nevertheless, the theater steadily lost ground until in 1954 no play other than *Jedermann* was performed. Again Lothar remedied the situation with a magnificent performance of Schiller's *Kabale und Liebe*. Fritz Schuh blazed the trail for contemporary drama with the first performance in German of O'Neill's *A Touch of the Poet*. The opera repertory is still dominated by Mozart and Strauss, but since 1947, when the world première of Gottfried von Einem's *Dantons Tod* took place, modern opera has had a firm place in the repertory.

In 1957 Herbert von Karajan became artistic director of the Salzburg Festival. He has added an Italian accent (Verdi's *Falstaff* and *Don Carlos* with stars of La Scala), engaged orchestras from Berlin, Amsterdam, and Paris, and added chamber opera to the program (Haydn's *Die Welt auf dem Monde*, Mozart's *La finta gardinera*). Although von Karajan resigned as artistic director in 1960, he will again participate in the Festival as a conductor.

It is surprising that the largest Festival audiences are not found in Salzburg, but in Bregenz, during its annual "Plays on the Lake." Here, in a marine theater, the Viennese operetta has experienced a vigorous revival since 1946 under the former director of the Burgtheater, Adolf Rott. Now that Bregenz also has a permanent stage, the Theater am Kornmarkt, the Festival offers drama to an international clientele in the best tradition of the Burgtheater.

Graz, the capital of Styria and a city which was greatly affected— adversely—by the dismemberment of the Austro-Hungarian Monarchy, conducted its first Festival week a few months after World War II. In 1948 the Grazer Festival Community was founded. In 1950 the Schlossbergbühne reopened with Richard Strauss's seldom heard *Friedenstag,* which had its world première in Munich in 1938. Grand opera, traditionally *Fidelio,* occupies a permanent place in the repertory, but contemporary works are staged every year. Like the other summer festivals in Austria, the Festspiel in Graz makes skillful use of historical buildings. Renaissance and baroque drama—in 1960 it was Jakob Bidermann's *Cenodoxus*— are performed in the courtyard of the Renaissance Landhaus; chamber music and ballet in beautiful Eggenberg Castle.

The geographical antipode to the Bregenz Festival, in Austria's Far West, is the lake festival on the shores of Lake Neusiedl, which forms part of the border between Austria and Hungary. Here, in the province where Franz Liszt was born 150 years ago, and where gypsy *bandas* still enliven every major celebration, the *Zigeunerbaron, Gräfin Mariza,* and *Viktoria und ihr Husar* are performed with zest and authenticity. Burgenland also has a wonderful natural stage in the deep moat of Forchtenstein Castle, where Goethe's *Götz von Berlichingen* and Franz Grillparzer's *Die Ahnfrau* are regularly performed.

Since 1951 the Vienna Festival offers at the end of the regular season, but still overlapping it, a tremendously rich program of opera, operetta, and drama; philharmonic, chamber, and choral concerts; serenatas, exhibitions, congresses, and symposia. For four weeks all theatrical and musical institutions, museums, and libraries strive to make Vienna a true summer festival. They are assisted by numerous foreign orchestras, choral groups, theatrical ensembles, and world-famous instrumentalists, vocalists, and conductors. In 1960 Egon Hilbert, the man who steered the Staatsoper through the stormy years of its reconstruction after World War II, became director of the Festival. During the celebration of 1961 all the stages in the city cooperated in a series of new productions paying tribute to the idea of freedom in its various contexts and dimensions. Visiting companies, among them the Helen Hayes ensemble, presented plays with the same general theme.

During the decennial of the Vienna Festival (1960), the Pawlatschen, a crude open-air stage symbolic of the old folk theater, was revived with a performance of Adolf Bäuerle's *Die falsche Prima-donna in Krähwinkel*. In 1962 the Vienna Festival had its own Festspielhaus, the venerable Theater an der Wien, where *Fidelio* was originally performed before an audience full of Napoleonic officers, where the Viennese operetta started its triumphant journey to all parts of the world, and where for ten years the Staatsoper was housed. The restoration of the Theater an der Wien and the modernization of its technical plant cost approximately 80 million Austrian shillings, or well over 3 million dollars.

The Burgtheater and the Staatsoper were, until 1918, court institutions. Since the dismemberment of the Austro-Hungarian Monarchy the Republic of Austria has operated these stages as federal, or national, theaters. The reconstruction of the Burgtheater and of the Opera cost more than 17 million U.S. dollars. In 1961 the expenses for these theaters and their affiliated stages were budgeted at more than 225 million Austrian shillings; this is more than the funds allocated to the Austrian Ministry of Foreign Affairs for its entire operation. At the end of 1961 the box-office receipts were estimated at approximately 70 million Austrian shillings. The deficit—155 million shillings—was covered with tax money.

What about the private theaters? These, too, at least in part, are government-supported. In Austria the theater is considered a cultural, not a business, enterprise. It is expected to reach people from all walks of life. If it is to fulfill its role a visit to the theater must be within reach of even the lowest-income groups. This is possible only with subsidies from all three levels of government. Few theaters cover more than 40 percent of their expenses by box-office receipts. In Vienna all of the private theaters, including the experimental stages, receive financial help from the federal government and/or the city of Vienna. The city disburses these subsidies from funds created by the *Kulturgroschen,* a small excise tax on movie tickets. During the season of 1960–1961 the city disbursed subsidies in the amount of 8,954,420 shillings to the three largest private theaters (Theater in der Josefstadt, Volkstheater, and Raimundtheater) and 400,000 shillings to the city's experimental stages.

All the large theaters in the *Länder,* or "states" in American terminology, are subsidized by the municipalities and/or state governments, and to a smaller degree also by the national government, more specifically, by the Austrian Ministry of Education. In 1961 the city of Graz and the Province of Styria each covered 50 percent of the deficit of 23 million Austrian shillings (almost a million dollars) incurred by their theaters. Another 3.5 million shillings was contributed by the Austrian Ministry of Education. The Schauspielhaus in Graz is being rebuilt at a cost of more than 55 million shillings. The new Festspielhaus in Salzburg was built by the federal government for a sum equivalent to 9 million U.S. dollars. During 1960–1961 the deficit of the Landestheater in Salzburg, almost 7 million shillings, was met by the city, state, and federal governments. For the Festival in 1961 the state of Salzburg contributed more than 4 million, the federal government almost 10 million shillings. The situation in other provinces or states is similar.

In addition to the subsidies of the theaters, the federal government and some of the *Länder* award prizes and scholarships to young playwrights and accomplished authors. The federal government also makes awards to managers of theaters who produce world premières of works by Austrian playwrights or who present especially meritorious productions of any work that has not been produced for two years or more.

In the final analysis, of course, it is still the Austrian taxpayer, regardless of whether he is a theatergoer, who has to pay the costs. That he does so willingly is proof that Austria's theater is not merely a tradition, but that it is still very much alive and steadily growing in importance, that it is an institution in which all Austrian citizens feel pride and interest.

German Drama and the American Stage

FRANCIS HODGE

# German Drama and the American Stage

FRANCIS HODGE

The question for consideration is simply this: What are we doing about producing German plays in this country?

The quick answer is: not very much. We are not concerned here with those plays put on by language departments in German. They are highly commendable for many reasons, not the least of which is their use as lively, entertaining devices to help students find the interior of the language and to give them some notion of the best plays in German, the same approach used by the English schoolboy to learn Latin back in the sixteenth century and to which the beginnings of modern English drama were tied. The subject under discussion here is the production of German plays, Swiss and Austrian as well as German, in English, which is a very different matter. During the past decade the professional Broadway theater, as far as I can determine, has shown only three such plays: Friedrich Dürrenmatt's *The Visit*, Fritz Hochwälder's *The Strong Are Lonely*, and Karl Wittlinger's *Do You Know the*

*Milky Way,* brought in from the Vancouver Festival. Only *The Visit* was successful. Off Broadway, where financially risky ventures are more feasible, four more have been produced: Schiller's *Mary Stuart,* Gresseiker's *Royal Gambit,* and two Brecht plays, *The Good Woman of Setzuan* and *The Threepenny Opera.* For a ten-year period this total is not very good.* Such paucity in the American production of German plays is vastly out of proportion to the German use of American plays and to the large fund of knowledge we have gained from the Germans about stage production, design, and the concept of theatrical theater. The Germans have been pioneering teachers in these areas, and our debt to them is tremendous. I should like to discuss here this far-reaching and highly creative aspect of the German contribution to the American stage, but I have decided that the transfer of German plays to American audiences is the more important subject for review, simply because it is more elusive, more controversial, more in need of our understanding. If what I have to say seems overly personal, too full of arguable opinions, it is so because this subject is highly complex and devoid of clear-cut solutions. Stage directors seldom venture to discuss it because the answers must too often depend on generalization, oversimplification, and personal opinion. But I think it is a theater problem we greatly need to understand better. The situation in New York during the past decade supports this opinion. The professional stage, however, is not the whole story. Another aspect of theater in America can no longer be pushed aside as a peripheral activity: I mean the "educational theater."

First, my own credentials. I am not an authority on German theater or drama. I do not speak the language, although I became somewhat acquainted with it as an undergraduate—with just enough reading of Goethe, Lessing, Schiller, and Heine to make me aware of another vast world of literature and culture that I despaired of ever getting in touch with unless I could use the language more directly. I did not achieve this linguistic facility. But I have come to some appreciation of this other cultural world in another way—as a teacher of theater history, who must place broad

* Since the Symposium New York has seen not only new productions of plays by Bertolt Brecht, but also two new plays by Max Frisch.

emphasis on the world's dramatic literature, and as a stage director, who must face the practical problems of meeting an audience.

My work has been in educational theater, that vast network of college and secondary school amateur theaters in this country which, together with community theaters, is estimated to number as high as 35,000 producing groups. Such a highly organized theater, tied to the school system not only by the production of plays but by the academic curriculum, exists in no other country in the world. I have worked with forty to fifty leading colleges and universities that make theater a major study in the curriculum, and in recent years with that even smaller group of universities tied directly to the professional theater by training students for it.

Formal training of this sort has been under way in a few universities for about forty years, and on the University of Texas campus, in this "professional" sense, for about half that time. This movement is therefore still young, and its influences are only beginning to be felt. What is at first noticeable are the remarkable theater plants on university campuses throughout the country. Many of these are in the million-dollar class and are equipped with major stages, workshops, experimental stages, elaborate lighting systems, and all the latest theater devices. The new theater center on this campus is directly in line with this national trend in developing materials. But though these physical assets, urgently needed, will greatly further the work that can be done, they cannot possibly be ends in themselves. A theater can be only as strong as the creative imaginations working within it, not only those who make the theater but those who witness it—the audience. Theater in the abstract does not exist; the creative audience in communication with the creative playwright, actor, designer, and director makes actual theater.

Theater activity of this sort in the university can be justified only on the basis of its ability to fulfill the principal functions of a university—preserving the best of the cultural past while advancing the present and looking with ideas to the future. But beyond preserving, recording, and investigating literary and graphic materials, the theater in the university has the art-museum function of staging live productions of the best plays of the past

71

as well as those of the present—it becomes literally a museum of theater art—and of giving leadership and direction to the new theater of our day. If the university is state-supported, the public responsibility is not unlike that of the famed city and state theaters in Munich, Hamburg, Berlin, and Vienna. The only difference is in the level of acting—the student actor against the seasoned professional; the supervisory staffs in the top university theaters are as professional in every respect as those in German state theaters.

This production function in the university has led to the development of a highly specialized drama-theater curriculum which affords training to students who will carry on not only the vast educational theater and the community theater allied to it, but also professional theater activities. The professional stage in America has become so infiltrated with university-trained people that a few years more will see it almost entirely in the hands of university products—playwrights, actors, designers, and directors. The educational responsibility of the university theaters, then, is enormous, and without strong and sure direction could lead to a worsening of theater in this country rather than an improvement. How to submit the creative artist to the university disciplines and, instead of fettering him, free his spirit and mature him so he can range more widely—that is the question the conscience of educational theater leadership is constantly examining. The answer will continue to lie in the creative and intellectual life within the theater centers which provide the background.

I have taken some time to note the position from which I speak because I believe it has much to do with the production of German plays in this country. Since educational theater is a germinal source, we can pertinently consider the quality of its creative life. We have some specific evidence. A look at the programming in 1950 and then again today will give us some indication of what the general trend is and will tell us specifically what role German drama plays in our theater.

A poll of 126 colleges and universities in 1950 revealed that forty-three schools produced nothing but Broadway successes, giving point to the old charge that the university theater is mainly an amateur adjunct of Broadway theater. Of the 403 productions reported, over 85 percent were American and English plays, includ-

72

ing about 8 percent devoted to the Shakespearean repertory. A dominance of English-language plays should be expected, but this high percentage leaves little room for any other drama. The significant point here is that less than 15 percent were drawn from the Continental repertory. And who was represented by more than a single production in this category? Only one playwright was on the list from each of five dramatically significant countries: Spain (Sierra), Hungary (Molnár), Russia (Gogol), Norway (Ibsen), and Italy (Casella). France was represented by three: Molière, Rostand, and Anatole France. *No German playwright was listed.* Not until we look at a series of isolated single performances do we discover that Brecht's *The Good Woman of Setzuan* was produced at Vassar. Other single productions of Continental plays were given, but the number was extremely small.

This poor showing should alert us, especially since most schools reported in the questionnaire for this study that their "chief concern [was] in providing a program which is educationally and culturally significant." How could they achieve this aim without representing an area of primary concern in our daily political life, namely Western Europe?

Such a discouraging report of the production of European drama in university theaters in 1950 prompted me, as I prepared this paper, to consider the present situation. Would it turn out to be the same as that for the professional theater? In an article in the *London Observer* on October 1, 1961, drama critic Kenneth Tynan, lately the critic on loan to *The New Yorker* and the most outspoken of the London play reviewers, reported in an article titled "The Breakthrough that Broke Down" that of thirty-four playhouses only three were staging plays that were written more than ten years ago, and that the oldest play in London, with three exceptions, was Agatha Christie's *The Mousetrap.* "I am for modernity," he writes, "but this is ridiculous." A decade ago, he continues, the London theaters were full of claptrap, worn-out forms, overweight musicals, and unreviewable revues, and the same is true today.

And what is the situation in New York? In the first week in November of 1961 a New York playgoer could see twenty-two productions on Broadway, but out of this small number—and note this—only nine were straight plays; the rest were musicals. Without off-Broadway production (nineteen plays on the same date) the straight play in New York would be almost a thing of the past. Would a new look at the university theaters turn out to be as depressing as the view of what is going on in the professional theaters in London and New York?

My poll was smaller and more highly selective than the 1950 review, for I wanted to find out what was happening at the top. About forty colleges and universities, representing most of the major state and private institutions, were included. They were geographically distributed among the states. Most were large institutions, but a few small ones were included for balance. This time the picture looked quite different. No school reported a program made up of Broadway successes; quite the contrary. All included at least one Continental European play. Of the 163 plays scheduled, 100 were American and English plays, this number including fourteen productions of Shakespeare, six of Shaw, and seventeen of new plays. Eight Classical Greek plays were also scheduled. The remainder—fifty-five plays or 34 percent—were Continental. Here is the breakdown:

| | | |
|---|---|---|
| French | 24 | (7 Molière, 5 Anouilh, Beckett, Claudel, Ionesco) |
| Italian | 7 | (4 Pirandello) |
| German | 13 | (6 Brecht, 3 Dürrenmatt, Gresseiker, Schnitzler, Kaiser, and a stage version of a Kafka novel) |
| Miscellaneous | 11 | (Spanish, Norwegian, etc.) |

Now this is quite a different use of German plays from that noted in 1950. Next to Shakespeare and Molière, Brecht ties with Shaw as the most-produced playwright on the list. But we should also note that the German theater, in contrast with the English, French, and Greek theaters, is not represented by classical drama. The poll also significantly discloses that no play in 1961 was produced on numerous stages as were *Our Town, Arsenic and Old Lace,* and other American and English plays in 1950. Rather, the number of different titles listed is very large, indicating that the total program was much more diverse.

If I seem overly enthusiastic about this shift toward Continental plays, I do not intend to imply that our theaters would be healthier if we eliminated musical comedies and wrote and produced far fewer American plays. It takes all kinds of plays to build a strong theater. And we must do everything we possibly can to encourage new American playwrights and plays. What I do want to suggest is that the balance in 1950 was not conducive to the growth and strengthening of the educational theater, and that the 1961 poll indicates a much greater concern in providing an educationally and culturally significant program. It also suggests that plays with higher intellectual content are being produced. But perhaps of most importance is the indication that the increased interest in European plays reflects a shift in this country from insularity to a world view, as Americans become awesomely aware that what happens to the rest of the world decidedly affects our own life at home. Out of all this one would like to hope that the shift in pro- gramming reflects a growing venturesomeness in university audi- ences and producers, a more independent spirit that could lead them away from the tried and sure into experiments with new forms and fresh ideas. It has been proved over and over again that only by adventuring in the theater arts can individuals in an audi- ence ever achieve a genuine theater experience. A greater respect for the art of the theater may be growing in this country.

But this growth can continue only as we adventure further. Our use of German plays is such a venturesome step. Yet suppose the audience is willing to venture, and the producer-director gathers enough courage for the plunge—what does he face when he tackles German drama? There can be no question of its value as a humanistic study, for plays, if rightly presented, can break down cultural barriers and broaden provincial views, because they give us identification with other peoples, who, except for language, are like ourselves. If the major problem of our day is how to avoid world catastrophe, some understanding of the views of others is absolutely necessary. Even though the idealistic approach to Ger- man plays is accepted many problems await solution in the process of transfer to the American stage.

The language barrier may be the least difficult to cope with. It is common to other languages, even English in its dialect forms.

One of the popular London successes of recent years, *Billy Liar*, a Yorkshire-dialect comedy, sounds to many Americans as if written in a foreign language. Brendon Behan's *The Hostage* when played by an Irish company is equally difficult to understand. What does a genuine Texas play about ranch life, spoken in pure Texese, sound like to a New England farmer? Could he hear it? Even if he could, would he comprehend it? Could he understand the interior action with all of its implications?

The transfer of ideas, solidly embedded as they so often are in social customs and environment, seems to be a far greater problem.

Somehow Pirandello has gotten through to us, as have Lorca and Chekhov. Ibsen has been more elusive, it seems to me, precisely because he is more Germanic. We have had no particular problem with French plays, and their transfer has been continuously in demand. Is it merely the French admiration for dramatic art that has made it the peak of literary achievement and that has brought most of the important French plays to New York and the schools? Certainly Paris, in contrast to New York and London, is the only city in the world where the supply of plays regularly on the stage, historical and modern, is so great that even the most avid playgoer has selection problems. Is it the French sense of adventure in dramatic art that in the last few years has developed a new shift in the theory of the play, and with it has given American producers a whole shelf of new plays for choice—from Anouilh to Genet to Beckett to Ionesco? Do the French have a certain objectivity that enables them to escape their cultural barriers more easily than other Europeans and to make their problems our problems too? Has the German too long been tied to his own history and cultural tradition and reflected them too confiningly in his theories of art and aesthetics to make communication easy? The fact remains that, with the exception of Paul Claudel, we have seen most of the contemporary French drama, but we have not had this wide contact with the German.

It is probably an oversimplification to say that we have been out of tune with German plays because the Germans and we have had different notions of what a play should be, but at least part of the answer lies in this approach. Back in 1857 Ibsen, in an essay on Scandinavian folk poetry, developed the thesis that a sharp cleavage existed between the North and the South European's characteristic attitude toward art. He argued that the Southerner, and by this he seems to mean principally the Italian, was content with a purely contemplative attitude, while the Northerner primarily sought a stimulus for exercising his own creative imagination and talent, that the Germanic peoples were receptive only to those arts which allowed freest play to the creative imagination. The Northerner, Ibsen maintained, does not yearn for the completed object, but prefers an outline sketch of the picture in order to put on the finishing touches himself in response to his own needs; unlike the Southerner he does not want the author to point to his own work and show up its center.

This theory of "incentive to individual creative activity," as Ibsen defined it, seems still to have validity, and can help us in delineating American-German differences. I suspect that Americans are closer to Ibsen's Southerner. We seem to need plays spelled out in more obvious, more direct terms. The notion that a play is an entertainment in which a story, literally and simply interpreted, is its only value and is complete in itself, has long been a popular American notion of theater. "When I go to a play," some say, "I don't want to be made to think or to get into the troubles of the everyday world; I want diversion." Is the theater art intended only to soothe, to mollify, to simply divert attention away from the world in which we live? Americans think they have a great taste for comedy, but how can really good comedy exist without the intellectual process? The perception of incongruities is its very life. Do not these people mean rather that they do not wish to have discussed in the theater, even in comedy, those subjects in which our guilts and responsibilities run deepest? It would be too gross a generalization to say that Americans cannot face realities, yet it is evident that many find them hard to face in an art form where emotional involvement occurs. On the other hand, those who hold that the theater should have intellectual content find it hard to use the theater only for simple diversion and not as our most potent public art device for getting at life and its meanings.

If there is validity in the argument that German drama is a heavier, more intellectual theater than the bulk of American plays have been in the past—and of course many exceptions qualify this oversimplification, of which the most obvious is Eugene O'Neill—how can the transfer problem be solved? What is the educational theater doing to help the situation?

Here at the University of Texas we have two levels of play production: a major bill of plays open to the public, and a more or less closed workshop laboratory program. Most of the major universities have similar arrangements. Through these two programs we have been able on this campus to give something of an emphasis to German plays. On our major bill we produced Brecht's *Mother Courage* in 1956, Dürrenmatt's *The Visit* in 1960, and Brecht's *The Good Woman of Setzuan* in 1961. The experimental workshop program has been far more varied, for here it is unnecessary to concern ourselves with audience likes and dislikes. The first level of production in this category—the Master's thesis—is fully staged in costume, setting, lighting, often experimentally with space-staging techniques. In this program we have produced Büchner's *Woyzeck* and Hauptmann's *The Beaver Coat*. The second level is devoted completely to new plays by our student playwrights. In our third level of workshop productions, a weekly presentation of scenes fully acted and directed but without costumes and with only basic set devices, we have ranged much more widely. In an attempt to give some concentration to German plays we have recently staged scenes from Hauptmann's *The Rats;* Sternheim's *The Snob;* Feuchtwanger's *Prisoners of War;* Kaiser's *Fire in the Opera House;* Hebbel's *Maria Magdalena;* Wedekind's *Earth Spirit;* and Toller's *Hinkemann.* There are many uses of such a production laboratory, not the least of which is permitting study of German plays and other similar bodies of dramatic literature in order to discover, if possible, whether they could be presented to a university audience and, if so, how best to offer them.

One of the principal problems in considering the production of German drama is that of adequate translations. Professor Eric Bentley has performed an important service here. In his freshly conceived anthologies of European drama he has revised our whole concept of what is available for classroom study and, more important, for live-theater production. He has not only brought us Brecht in translation, but also, as editor and adapter, he has reintroduced us to a number of other German works. But it takes many hands to provide us with a body of usable plays. Except for *Faust,* and a very few others, the German classical drama is simply not available in "theater" English. Unless a stage director is highly enough motivated, as well as capable of preparing new acting versions, he is cut off from most of Goethe, Schiller, Kleist, Lessing, and others. Büchner has fared somewhat better, with the result that both *Woyzeck* and *Dantons Tod,* perhaps more modern in spirit and style, have found occasional productions, as the former has here. Two new versions of Schiller's *Mary Stuart,* Eric Bentley's and the translation prepared for Tyrone Guthrie's New York production, played throughout the country by Eva Le Gallienne, are available for university staging. This play is an exciting adventure in intrigue and character psychology, and its historical English setting gives it appeal for American audiences. Such version preparations are very much the work of a university theater, but they are not prepared without great difficulties. When Lillian Hellman had finished adapting Anouilh's *The Lark* for the successful Broadway staging with Julie Harris, she said she would never undertake adaptation again because it was more difficult than writing a new play of her own. There can be no question that the success of German plays in this country is determined by the quality of the American-English versions used. Here is a vast area for the student of German. But knowing the language and the author is scarcely enough. The ideal adapter—a translator is not enough—must have a poet's awareness of language, a high understanding of dramatic action and its relation to character, a theater craftsman's knowledge of dialogue and construction, and a subtle feeling for mood and theater ideas. He should, in other words, be a playwright himself. There are reasons for Anouilh's success in English when Christopher Fry and Lillian Hellman do the adapting.

Adapters of recent plays encounter also the entanglement of rights and royalties. Plays can be highly valuable properties and need the strongest legal protection. Yet unless they are somehow made more readily available to capable adapters, as Brecht's plays have been, the high value of their immediacy will pass before we see them. Mordecai Gorelik, the stage designer, theater historian, and theorist, who has done much to promote German theater in this country as one of the earliest to recognize Brecht's important innovations, told me that in two recent instances when he tried to obtain translation rights he was discouraged by a one-year limitation on the translation and by a demand for advance royalties. Such procedures do not greatly encourage the transfer of German plays into English.

Good translations alone are not enough to urge us to present German historical drama. American directors need to be shown more about how to produce these plays so constantly in the modern German repertory, and especially how to act them. German acting companies, like the one which toured Argentina in 1961, performing among other plays Schiller's *The Robbers*, should visit America, as French and English companies do, to show us their interpretation of German classical drama on the stage. With examples before us we can better find our own ways of adapting it. As New York in the last decade has seen the Comédie Française, Jean Louis Barrault's company, and the Théâtre National Populaire, and as the University of Texas campus saw the Vieux Colombier company for several seasons, so should we also see companies from Berlin, Hamburg, Munich, Vienna, and Zurich. They have performed in Paris; why can they not come to this country? Despite the language barrier the French productions in the United States reached out and touched our audiences with the power of their great plays. German companies could be equally successful. As an American travelling in Germany I was much impressed with the acting in the state and city-operated theaters, and particularly by what seemed to be taken for granted, the large number of mature male actors capable of performing master roles. Our American actors in a theater greatly devoted to youthful actors and audiences could learn much by watching such companies in action. And we very much need to see the classical German drama performed by German actors. It is hoped that the Lincoln Center Theater project in New York will take a strong leadership in this direction.

With the impetus of fresh versions and more production know-how, we should be inevitably in a better position to make the transfer in our own terms. But what are these terms? American theatergoers seem to want—perhaps they even need, for understanding—a high degree of contemporaneity in the production of historical plays, that is, obvious pertinence of the ideas in a play to our times or to our American tradition. In the theater production of the 1960's, with its highly diverse use of styles, historical plays must exist as theater and not as history: *Julius Caesar* in modern dress; *Troilus and Cressida* in Civil War background; *As You Like It* in a modern jazz context. Whether or not we agree with this approach, it has become a prevailing mode. We have no Comédie Française to support a style of acting in historical plays differing from the current manner, or to prepare us for a kind of dramatic museum piece. Without German history and tradition as support, without strong aesthetic ties with the past, what can Americans find in *Egmont, Götz von Berlichingen, Nathan the Wise, The Robbers,* or *The Prince of Homburg,* the historical dramas that German young people are brought up on? The great difficulty is in finding in them what is beyond pure story—political awareness, for example—that could excite our imaginations. If we are to do them at all, we must find that note of transfer in the adaptations, and in the acting and production. This is a master repertory of Romantic drama that we should learn how to use. We cannot escape the fact that in England and America we do not produce our own Romantic plays of the same period. A long, barren gap of one hundred years exists between Sheridan and Shaw, for we have not discovered what to do with the huge body of available English plays belonging to this period. The success of Schiller's *Mary Stuart* in this country should alert us not only to possibilities with the German repertory, but also to what can be done with our own nineteenth-century plays.

When we turn to the post-Ibsen period of German plays we are immediately confronted with that much-heard generalization that they are too heavy for American tastes. Speculation of what this means can go in many directions, but I wonder if it does not derive partly from those common folk-myth images the American has of German life, much of which has been spread by the Germans themselves in their caricatures and satires on German life, and partly from what the American has seen or heard of German taste in music, architecture, and painting. By "heavy" plays I suspect such critics mean that they incline to seriousness, to a certain amount of intellectual content, to philosophical statement, and to a picturing of the darker though more realistic aspects of life. This is the world of Ibsen and Strindberg, but it is also that of Wedekind, Kaiser, and Toller.

Most Americans nowadays, if they know anything at all about German plays, have probably read the Expressionists, but they have not seen them on the stage. It is quite probable that our notion of German drama is based largely on ignorance. Hauptmann's image has been more a reflection of the high seriousness of *The Weavers* and *The Sunken Bell* than of the paradoxical, ironic, often amusing dialect pieces of Berlin life in *The Rats* and *The Beaver Coat*. Altogether we have seen very little of this major writer. There is probably much truth in Dürrenmatt's thesis that audience tastes have moved away from highly serious drama to the avenue of comedy, no matter how bitter, cynical, and sardonic it may be. How readily serious American playgoers are following the new directions in the plays of the avant gardists, stemming largely as they do from European nihilistic philosophies emerging out of the European upheaval of the last few decades, is difficult to know. But one thing is certain: German Expressionistic drama is as dead here as it is in Germany, except in the university theater workshops —for example, the production of Kaiser's *The Coral* at Tulane— where it still has historical value, and where Wedekind and Toller can still excite. Some of the ideas in these plays might still seem radical to American audiences, but their highly serious style disqualifies their general use. But what has not been lost are the theater techniques they engendered. We learned much about the theatrical theater from these plays.

German comedies have a better chance. And here is where the Austrian and Swiss influences are strongly felt. Schnitzler's *Anatol* plays have been rumored for an off-Broadway musical. A Nestroy satire such as *Liberty Comes to Krähwinkel* could probably find favor just as Thornton Wilder's *The Matchmaker*, adapted from another Nestroy farce, already has. Carl Sternheim's satirical comedies have a very possible chance of acceptance, if we can get them acted. His *1913* certainly could not have the satiric meanings it must have for Germans today in its West German revival, but it still has much to carry it. *The Snob* and *The Mask of Virtue* both have possibilities as light comedies. Of recent writers, Americans await more from the Swiss playwrights Friedrich Dürrenmatt and Max Frisch. Carl Zuckmayer's *The Devil's General* was seen in a London production, but has not been shown in this country.

It is Bertolt Brecht, as noted in the university theater program poll, who is the most frequently produced German playwright in America. I should like to examine his *The Good Woman of Setzuan* here from a production point of view. This is the most frequently produced Brecht play in America. What do we see in it? Let me warn you that I am now going to tread on the highly personal ground of play interpretation. What I think about this play may be different from what you may think about it. But no matter what point of view either of us holds, the transfer problems are still there. What can we do with the form and ideas in *The Good Woman* that will help it reach our university audience? What are the specific problems of transfer?

To help reveal these problems more clearly I am going to contrast *The Good Woman* with *The Skin of Our Teeth,* American playwright Thornton Wilder's fantastic comedy about man's age-old struggle to survive. Both plays were written about the same time: the Brecht in 1938–1940, when he was living in the United States, the Wilder in 1942, and both have met the critics in New York productions, with the 1955 revival of *The Skin of Our Teeth* on the stage just one year before Eric Bentley staged *The Good Woman* at the Phoenix Theater. Both have been seen widely in Europe, with the Wilder in a German version as well as in the English original as played by the Helen Hayes-Theater Guild company all over the Continent in 1961. A minor historical point that brings Wilder and Brecht together was Brecht's suggestion that the American playwright do an English version of *The Good Woman*. Had Wilder done this, we would have had a unique example of major American and German playwrights in collaboration.

Now a major point in this comparison is the likeness of these two plays in form. Both are parable plays, in that they tell relatively simple stories with the object of setting out some philosophy or moral about man. Both are innovations in their departures from the highly conventional form of realism. In the Wilder, man is blind and foolish but means well; he tries to profit from the past; he loses faith, manages to escape disasters by the skin of his teeth, helped by the practical common sense of women, picks up, and struggles on. Brecht's man is not drawn on such a wide, historical scale. He is mean, petty, lost. In his blindness and idealism he destroys his fellow man as quickly with soft handouts as he does with ruthless exploitation. Man's existence lies somewhere between these extremes, and man can change the world only by gradually achieving this median good. There is even a similar scene in the two plays as Mr. Antrobus in Wilder's play and Shen Te in Brecht's deal with the problems of what to do with the poor and homeless. And both plays use the theatrical devices of direct address to the audience, interruptions for speeches or songs, overt philosophical statements by either gods or philosophers. Both use the physical stage not as an exact place, but as a suggested reality.

The dissimilarities between these plays are equally obvious. *The Skin of Our Teeth* is frequently characterized as a comic vaudeville show, a lively theater joke, a supreme novelty. We follow Mr. Antrobus, inventor of the wheel, through the coming of the Ice Age, when he big-heartedly offers food and shelter to animals and refugees; to a convention in Atlantic City, where he is puffed up with pride and prosperity, covetous, lecherous, and forgetful of his conjugal duties; and home to pull his family together again after the destruction of the war. Mr. Wilder's method is to present his satiric and essentially hopeful history of mankind through the façade of comic contrivance, to slip the audience a serious message, and to keep them in the theater through a series of high jinks and a few serious moments. To Americans his homey type characters, his picture of American family life, and his setting of the play in the realistic façade of life in New Jersey and Atlantic City is completely familiar. This façade is part of us and the story is readily absorbed. But the transfer of ideas, relatively simple though they may be, is not as easy as it would seem with American audiences.

When *The Skin of Our Teeth* was first seen in New York in 1942 it became the controversial play of the season as it impressed through its innovations, bored and confused that part of the audience who looked for a story play, awed and fascinated those who found its ideas unusual. How many in the popular audience thoroughly understood what was going on in the play is one of those unanswerable questions. The critical reception of the 1955 revival was mixed, although largely favorable. But a negative attitude was more openly expressed than in 1942. Wilder was characterized as a serious-minded teacher trying to frolic with his students, and the play was deemed just as sophomoric, as windy, and as irritating as in 1942, with its wisdom strictly inadequate. One reviewer thought it an anachronistic, utterly baffling allegory; and another quoted Tallulah Bankhead, who had played Sabina in the 1942 production, as saying, "There is less to it than meets the ear." In Europe, according to American press reports of the Theater Guild tour, it met enthusiastic success, as it had in West German productions immediately after the War. Was it an easy play for Europeans with their tradition of idea-plays as background?

Now what can be said for *The Good Woman of Setzuan?* First, we are confronted with Brecht's tie to German Communism, a fact which can pose problems in understanding and interpreting certain parts of the play and which can color audience attitude. When we turn to the play, we find it has been variously described as a morality, a pseudo-Chinese drama, a cynical comedy, a collection of the odds and ends of outmoded German Expressionism, and a naive, childlike story for eleven-year-olds. Quite unlike Mr. Wilder in his vaudeville approach, Brecht tells his story in a more or less straightforward manner, but not without wry, cynical humor. The play has the ring of old-fashioned melodrama about it as we watch the unselfish, almost too good Shen Te being swallowed up by lazy and greedy hangers-on; as we see her fall in love with a good-for-nothing airplane pilot who jilts her when she refuses to hand over her money; as we watch her fight back behind the masquerade of a ruthless cousin, the concealment device she has arranged to protect herself, and confess this subterfuge in a public trial for the murder of her "good" self. To some critics this story seems trite and worn, and especially so if one sees Shen Te as a romantic prostitute with a heart of gold. But if she is viewed realistically as a woman who has been degraded from necessity, and who knows that ruthless expediency is the only way one can survive in a hard world, that it is not a sin to be poor but a cruel reality, the distinctive features of the play begin to emerge. Brecht's world here is one of poverty, of a low level of society, of petty shopkeepers and the homeless in a dog-eat-dog existence. It is full of meanness, of filthy food in garbage cans, of petty theft and sly double-dealing, of parents and their children betraying each other, of the injured without medical treatment, of the poor feeding on the poor, of a godless place of want and despair. This is the real world to Brecht because the bulk of humanity live in it.

Is Brecht talking only about man's expediency and meanness when he is poor, or does he rather suggest that most of mankind, no matter what his economic level may be, is morally corrupt? Shen Te at first tries to help others and improve this degraded world about her by generously giving what she has, but she soon sees that charity alone fails, that she weakens rather than strengthens mankind. When, as the ruthless cousin, she begins her hard exploitation of the workers, physical and material matters are improved; yet the evil of the subjection of the individual, the loss of the dignity of man is even worse than before. The strongest irony in this play is that love of another and love of humanity can possibly exist in this degraded world, that there is positive hope for goodness, the note on which Brecht ends his play.

I think you can readily see some of the problems. If *The Skin of Our Teeth* was difficult for some audiences to understand, what can they make of *The Good Woman?* First, instead of original English we must find Brecht's idea through the relay of an English version, with all its problems of interpreted meanings. Mr. Bentley, who introduced this play to Americans, has published two, of which the second is the shakedown product resulting from the hard grind of stage production and performance. Instead of the familiar American façade of Wilder's play, we are confronted with the strangeness of a Chinese city. But is it really Chinese? Could it not just as well be London, or New York, or Berlin? Instead of vaudeville comedy and high jinks we have a straightforward, wryly amusing, relatively simple story line. We are asked to pay the price of a theater ticket to watch man's loss of dignity in this real world of beggary, a subject we have seldom seen set out on the stage with such force and overt detail. In the America of 1961 there are some who even doubt that poverty exists, in spite of the fact that we are informed by reliable sources that one-third of the world's population has an annual family income of fifty to one hundred dollars. Brecht wrote his play in the late thirties in the context of the worst economic depression the world has ever known; in 1961 this is either remote or nonexistent to many in an audience. The subject matter seems so depressing that some theatergoers will take the same position as the *New York Mirror* critic who said in his review of Harold Pinter's *The Caretaker* when it opened in New York after a long run in London: "We just don't believe that drab mixed-up people make for stimulating or rewarding theater. We like our slice of life off the top and not the lowest stratum of humanity."

Another view holds, however, that the theater is a place for ideas and new forms. *The Good Woman* may not be the best of Brecht's plays, not as strong, bold, sharply satirical as others, but it clearly demonstrates the power of a parable in laying out an idea. You must merely believe in the sort of theater that discusses realities. Mr. Wilder in *The Skin of Our Teeth* keeps telling us what we are to do with his play. Brecht does not do this, but leaves us, in the German tradition, to unravel more for ourselves. A strange form, a strange locale, a strange idea—this is how Brecht seems to many Americans. *The Good Woman of Setzuan* looked little different to the New York critics when they reviewed the production in 1956. American critics are not supposed to be sociologists or even to display political awareness, but it is a sad commentary to note that not one even mentioned that Brecht's play had any relationship to a real world or that the subject of man's plight was of the slightest concern to anyone. They were reviewing a fairy tale they did not like; the nearest musical, in their view, apparently had a more significant story.

Producing Brecht is no easy task. It would be almost impossible to stage his plays in the highly detailed, moving-picture-like manner of the Berliner Ensemble, with its large company of highly competent actors who have won a reputation as the finest acting ensemble in Europe. Yet *The Good Woman* must have the most careful staging. How can student actors in an American university portray poverty and expedience with genuine conviction? What does the musical accompaniment for the songs sound like? Should it be pseudo-Chinese, or a simple melodic line in our Western style, or a satirical music-hall sound? Much must be done to give it the right theatrical setting, to obscure what to Americans seems too coy, too charming, too trite, in its use of the Chinese theater which attracted Brecht; to set out its world of poverty in a theatrical way so that our audience can recognize it as its own world today and not only that of a remote foreign world or of the depression years of the thirties; to find the right balance between tenderness and passion and the objective view that will bring the audience to a closer understanding of the world in which it lives. It must be designed as a play for home consumption. We must find the rhythm in which it moves, and set it out in theater terms that our audience can comprehend. But above all the audience must play its part. It must be sympathetic, with its sympathy that of a willingness to adventure into less familiar forms and ideas.

My thesis, then, is simply this: if we are to have more German plays on our American stage, we must develop a more adventurous attitude in the choice of plays and in fresh stagings, and the audience to receive them. Good English versions can certainly help, but we must first have a more solid tradition, a more sophisticated view of theater as a significant art form. The university theaters are moving in this direction. They may even be responsible for the new professional area theaters presently developing throughout the country. A hope for more German drama in America, then, is also a hope for a better, more durable, more necessary theater in this country. It means that we will be able to look further outside our own immediate world and, as an impetus to our maturing, see other peoples. If our own theater is strengthened by a new look at others, will America not present a better image abroad as a nation highly concerned, not entirely with its own immediate needs, but with the much larger pattern of man's destiny? All the art forms have the capability of crossing barriers if we let them, but theater inherently possesses the great capability of talking directly to us not only across the ages, but from languages and peoples in our own day. As public mirrors, plays can help untangle the Chinese knot we have tied in our modern civilization.

Epic Theater Is Lyric Theater

ERIC BENTLEY

# Epic Theater Is Lyric Theater[1]

## ERIC BENTLEY

Bertolt Brecht's Epic Theater has been described in so many abstruse and pretentious ways that I recently attempted a simplification in a formula: Epic Theater Is Lyric Theater. I was not serious beyond a certain point; I was using half-seriousness to demolish overseriousness. I do not "seriously" wish to discount the epic (or narrative) elements in Brecht's work, and I am not retracting what I myself have said about them in earlier years. I am saying that if Brecht's own paradox is permissible—that theater can lose the name "dramatic" and acquire the title "epic"—then it is equally permissible to call his nondramatic theater "lyric"—for three reasons: first, that Brecht started out as a lyric poet and later developed his lyrics into plays; second, that the lyrics in his

---

[1] One dimension of Eric Bentley's presentation will necessarily be missing from this book. Those of the poems which have been set to music he sang, accompanying himself at the piano. This dimension does survive, however, in the form of a tape-recording that has been broadcast by the University of Texas Radio Station. A similar performance has been put on disc by Riverside Records under the title *Bentley on Brecht*. [Ed.]

plays occupy a central, not a peripheral, position; and third, that, since the word *lyric* connotes the voice of the poet himself, and Brecht's works can be called, like Goethe's, "fragments of one long confession," then it may be instructive for the student of Brecht's *theater* to trace the development of Brecht the dramatist through the *poems* and *songs*, even though not all of these are found in the plays.

Since this is hardly the occasion for pure theory, what I shall attempt is a kind of self-portrait of Brecht, insofar as a portrait can be painted in words—and translated words at that. On the latter point I can only hope that my readers are interested in problems of translation, so that even when they cannot admire what I have made of Brecht's German, they may at least sympathize with my predicament. I rather think that a self-portrait, even in translation, will be more serviceable than any independent words of mine would be. I shall therefore keep my comments to a minimum.

Bertolt Brecht was born in 1898 in Augsburg, Bavaria.

## ABOUT POOR B.B.[2]
### *(Vom armen B.B.)*

I, Bertolt Brecht, come from the black forests.
My mother took me to the cities while I lay
Inside her. The coldness of the forests
Will be with me till my dying day.

The asphalt cities are my home. From the very first
They supplied me with every last sacrament:
Newspapers, tobacco, brandy—
Suspicious, lazy, and when all's said, content.

I am friendly with people. I stick
A stiff hat on my head as they do.
"They are beasts," I say, "with a particular odor."
"So what?" I also say, "I am too."

In the morning, sometimes, I take some girls and sit them
In my empty armchairs. Whereupon I
Look them nonchalantly over and declare:
"In me you have a man on whom you can't rely."

[2] Copyright © 1958 by the *Kenyon Review*.

Toward evening I gather some fellows around me.
We address each other as: "Gentlemen."
They put their feet up on my table and remark:
"Things will improve." I don't ask when.

Toward morning, in the grey of dawn, the pines are pissing
And their bugs, the birds, begin to weep.
In the city I empty my glass, throw away my cigar stub, and
Go unhappily to sleep.

We have been living, a light generation,
In houses that were thought beyond destruction.
(The lanky buildings of Manhattan Island and the fine antennae
That amuse the Atlantic Ocean are of our construction.)

Of these cities will remain that which blew through them: the wind.
A full pantry rejoices the guests: they eat it bare.
Our tenancy, we know, is transient. After us will follow
Nothing worth a dare.

As for the earthquakes to come, when they ask me if I
Will get bitter and let my cigar go out, I answer: No!
I, Bertolt Brecht, who came from the black forests
To the asphalt cities inside my mother long ago.

Bertolt Brecht was just old enough to be drafted into the German
army during World War I. He became a medical orderly. And
he wrote a poetic comment on the war which is said to have circulated among the soldiers, spreading a very healthy defeatism.

### BALLAD OF THE DEAD SOLDIER [3]
*(Legende vom toten Soldaten)*

When the fifth spring came and still the war
Made ne'er a pause for breath,
The soldier, who knew what a soldier's for,
Died a hero's death.

[3] The translation is shorter than the German by a couple of stanzas. Copyright
© 1958 by the *Kenyon Review*. This translation, like the others printed here, is
written to be sung to the same music as the German. Exceptional, in this respect,
are the translations of the three elegies: a different translation of Mr. Bentley's
has been made for use with Eisler's settings of these. [Ed.]

93

But war for battle is a synonym
And the Kaiser was most upset
That his soldier had gone and died on him.
He shouldn't have done that yet.

Without the Kaiser's permission, though,
The summer rolled in like a wave,
Then came a medical commission, oh,
To that young soldier's grave.

The medical commission said
A little prayer to their maker,
Which done, they dug with a holy spade
The soldier from god's little acre.

When the doctor examined the soldier gay
Or what of him was left,
He softly said: This man's 1-A,
He's simply evading the draft.

The soldier was then reinducted.
The night was blue and dry.
If one hadn't had a helmet on, one might have detected
The Fatherland's stars in the sky.

They filled him up with brandy
Though his flesh had putrefied,
And kept two nurses handy
And his half-naked wife at his side.

A priest led a handsome procession there,
And knowing corpses well
He swung some incense in the air
To cover up the smell.

Behind the priest there beat and blew
Trumpet and kettledrum.
Our soldier could do what he had to do:
He kicked out his legs from his bum.

Zing boom, zing boom, that was the sound
As down the dark streets they did go
And the soldier with them reeling round
Like a stormswept flake of snow.

The cats and dogs, they squeal and prance,
Rats whistle far and near,
For none could bear to belong to France
O fie! the mere idea!

The women came out to see the sight
In the villages near and far.
Trees bowed their heads and the moon shone bright
And everyone cried "hurrah!"

What shouts, what drums, what trumpet-peals,
Women and priestly flunkey!
And in the midst that soldier reels
Like a drunken monkey.

And up and down, and down and up,
They jostled him till soon
You just couldn't see him except from on top,
And there's no one there but the moon.

But the moon won't stay there the whole day through
For the sun won't pause for breath.
The soldier did what he'd been taught to do:
He died a hero's death.

LEGENDE VOM TOTEN SOLDATEN

Anon.

Und als der Krieg im fünf - ten Lenz kei - nen

Aus - blick auf Frie - den bot, da zog der Sol - dat sei - ne

Kon - se - quenz und starb den Hel - den - tod.

The "Ballad of the Dead Soldier" brings to mind Kurt Tuchol-sky's statement that Georg Grosz taught a whole generation to see their Germany. Brecht wrote a good deal in the Georg Grosz vein, but also a good deal in other veins.

First: Parody of Romance

### MEMORY OF MARIE A.
*(Erinnerung an die Marie A.)*

Upon that day, a day of blue September,
Silent and still beneath a young plum tree,
I held my silent, still, and pale belovèd
And in my arms a golden dream was she.
And in the wide and lovely summer heavens
There was a cloud, I saw it fleetingly.
It was pure white and, oh, so high above us!
When I looked up, it vanished suddenly.

And since that moment, many a September
Came sailing in, then floated down the stream.
The plum trees doubtless are no longer living
And if you ask: what happened to my dream
I shall reply: I cannot now remember,
Though what you have in mind I surely know.
And yet her face, I really don't recall it.
I just recall I kissed it long ago.

Even the kiss would have been long forgotten
If that white cloud had not been in the sky.
I know the cloud, and shall know it forever,
It was pure white and, oh, so very high.
Perhaps the plum trees still are there and living,
Perhaps by now the woman has six children too.
But that white cloud, it only lived one moment:
When I looked up, it vanished in the blue.

## ERINNERUNG AN DIE MARIE A.

Anon.

An je - nem Tag im blau - en Mond Sep -

tem - ber, Still un - ter ei - nem jung - en Pflau - men -

baum, Da hielt ich sie, die still - e blei - che

Lie - be, In meinem Arm wie einen holden

Traum. Und über uns im schönen Sonnen -

himmel War eine Wolke, die ich nicht lang

sah. Sie war sehr weiss und unge - heuer

oben, Und als ich aufsah war sie nimmer

da.

Second: Anal Humor

## ORGE'S HYMN [4]
### *(Orges Gesang)*

Orge said to me:

The dearest place on earth was not (he'd say)
The grassy plot where his dead parents lay;

Nor a confessional, nor harlot's bed,
Nor a soft lap, warm, white, and fat (he said).

The place which he liked best to look upon
In this wide world of ours was the john.

It is a place where we rejoice to know
That there are stars above and dung below.

A place where you can sit—oh wondrous sight—
And be alone even on your wedding night.

A place that teaches you (so Orge sings):
Be humble, for you can't hold on to things.

A place where one can rest and yet where one
Gently but firmly can get business done.

A place of wisdom where one has the leisure
To get one's paunch prepared for future pleasure.

And there you find out what you are indeed:
A fellow who sits on a john—to feed!

ORGES GESANG

Third: Pure Lyric

The following is a good poem to read, or sing, to people who
think of Brecht as a social poet, lacking in all sense of either individual being or of the cosmos around us.

### OF THE WORLD'S KINDNESS
*(Von der Freundlichkeit der Welt)*

To this earth whereon the winds are wild
Each of you came as a naked child.
Owning nothing, your body froze
When a woman gave you swaddling clothes.

No one called you. You were not besought.
In no handsome carriage were you brought.
On this earth you were quite unknown
When a man placed his hand in your own.

And to you the world can nothing owe.
If you want to, you can always go.
Though to you the many turned deaf ears,
Many too on your account shed tears.

From this earth whereon the winds are wild
You depart with scurf and scab defiled.
Almost all rejoice at their own birth
Long before they go back to the earth.

VON DER FREUNDLICHKEIT DER WELT

99

Fourth:  Unclassified

The last in this group of nonpolitical poems is one I do not know how to classify.  But this I do know:  here spoke a new voice in German poetry.

### EARLY MORNING ADDRESS TO A TREE CALLED "GREEN"
*(Morgendliche Rede an den Baum Green)*

I did you a bitter wrong tonight.
I could not sleep: so deafening was the wind.
When I looked out, I noticed you were staggering
Like a drunken monkey.  I was ashamed for you, Green.

Let me simply confess I was mistaken:
You were fighting the bitterest battle of your life.
Vultures were getting interested in you.
Now you know your worth, Green.

Today the yellow sun is shining on your naked boughs
But you're still shaking the tears off, aren't you, Green?
You're rather alone, aren't you, Green?
Mass civilization isn't for us, is it?

I was able to get some sleep after I'd seen you.
But you must feel tired today, no?
Forgive my idle chatter.
It was after all no small achievement to get up so high
Between the houses,
Up so high that the storm can reach you,
Green, like tonight.

The world knows Bertolt Brecht as a Communist.  Whether or not he ever belonged to the Communist Party—and he said he did not—, it is certain that in, or about, 1928 he was won over to those Marxist ideas which he continued to hold for the rest of his life. The following poem, however, was published in 1927.

### HYMN OF THE RED ARMY SOLDIER [5]
*(Gesang des Soldaten der roten Armee)*

Because beneath its leaden sun
This land of ours is eaten bare,
It spat us out on freezing highways,
It spat us out on byways dark.

[5] Copyright © 1961 by *Encounter*.

Though washed in snow until the spring,
The army is red summer's child.
The fall brought snow. When it was winter
The army's heart froze in the wind.

In those years Freedom was a word
That often fell from lips of ice,
And some had tiger's fangs that followed
After the red, inhuman flag.

And when by night the red moon swam
Our fellows tied their horses up.
And in the fields talked of the future,
Then fell asleep, tired by the march.

The rain it rained, the dark wind blew,
To sleep on stones was very sweet.
The rain removed from weary eyelids
Not the dirt only, but our sins.

And when at night the sky grew red
They took it for the red of dawn.
It was a fire; the dawn came later.
But Freedom never came, my boys!

And so wherever they might be
They said: This finally is hell.
But all the hells that once were final
Gave place to others finally.

So many hells were still to come.
But Freedom never came, my boys!
And now if what arrived were Heaven,
They would not be around to see.

When we ourselves are eaten bare
(Our hearts as leaden as the sun)
The army spits our skin and bones out
Into a hole not deep but cold.

With bodies hardened by the rain,
With hearts disfigured by the ice,
With empty, bloody hands and grinning,
We enter now *Your Paradise.*

## GESANG DES SOLDATEN DER ROTEN ARMEE

Weil un-ser Land zer-fres-sen ist mit ei-ner

mat-ten Son-ne drin, spie es uns aus in dunk-le

Stra-ssen und frie-ren-de Chaus-se-en hin.

The year 1928 was marked by the appearance of *The Three-penny Opera.* Here is a work which is so easily available both in print and on discs that I can largely ignore it here. I will content myself with quoting some verses which, strictly speaking, belong to the film version, but which are special favorites of all Brecht *aficionados.* The stanzas were added to "Die Moritat von Mackie Messer" and sung to Kurt Weill's famous tune. I'm afraid they are also untranslatable, so I will give the German also.

> Here it comes: the Happy Ending!
> Westward, look, the land is bright!
> When you've money in your pocket
> Things will usually come right.
>
> Smith accuses Jones of things which
> Only Smith may perpetrate.
> But the Ending's Happy when they
> Jointly rob the poor man's plate.
>
> Some are children of the darkness,
> Some are children of the sun.
> You can see the sons of sunshine.
> Sons of dark are seen by none.

102

Und so kommt zum guten Ende
Alles unter einen Hut.
Ist das nötige Geld vorhanden
Ist das Ende meistens gut.

Dass nur er im Trüben fische
Hat der Hinz den Kunz bedroht.
Doch zum Schluss vereint am Tische
Essen sie des Armen Brot.

Denn die einen sind im Dunkeln
Und die andern sind im Licht.
Und man siehet die im Lichte,
Die im Dunkeln sieht man nicht.

1929–1933. The Wall Street crash. World Depression. The rise of Hitler. Brecht's poem, "Faded Glory of the Giant City of New York," would be very *à propos,* but is too long for my presentation. Instead, here is a poem about the faded glory of his own country. Of the author of such a poem it might be said that he must either be converted to religion or to—Communism.

### DOOMED GENERATIONS
*(Gezeichnete Geschlechter)*

Long, long before the bombers appeared in our skies
Our cities were already
Uninhabitable.
No sewer drained off our garbage.
Long, long before we fell in the countless battles,
Still walking through our cities (which were still standing)
Our wives were already
Our widows,
And our children
Our orphans.
Long, long before they who themselves were doomed
Threw us in our graves,
We were already
Friendless.
Those bits of us that the quicklime ate away at
Were no longer
Faces.

The doomed generations. There is a Brecht poem in which the feeling of being doomed is seen in a different way—from the viewpoint of the innocent.

### SWARMS OF STARLINGS
*(Lied der Starenschwärme)*

We started out in the month of October
In the province of Suiyan.
Swiftly we flew, without detours, in a southerly direction,
Over four provinces, for five days.
> Fly faster! The plains are waiting!
> It's growing colder.
> The plains are warm.

We started out, eight thousand of us,
In the province of Suiyan.
Daily our numbers grew by the thousand the farther we flew
Over four provinces, for five days.
> Fly faster! The plains are waiting!
> It's growing colder.
> The plains are warm.

We are now flying over the plain
In the province of Hunan.
Nets, great nets, are what we see beneath us and we know
What we've been flying to, these five days.
> The plains have waited.
> It's growing warmer and
> Our death is certain.

1933. Brecht left Germany the day after the Reichstag fire. His own books were on a fire not long afterwards. He was now *an exile.*

## A VISIT TO THE EXILED POETS
*(Besuch bei den verbannten Dichtern)*

When in a dream he entered the hut of the exiled poets
Which is next to the hut where the exiled teachers live
(From the latter he heard quarrelling and laughter)
Ovid came to meet him in the doorway and said in an undertone:
"You'd better not sit down now, you're not dead yet. Who knows,
You might still go back, and without anything having
                                  changed, except you."
But with comfort in his eyes Po Chu-i approached and said
                                    with a smile:
"Anyone who has called injustice by its name as often as once
Gets what's coming to him. And his friend Tu Fu quietly added:
"Exile, you understand, is not a place where Pride is unlearned!"
Earthier than these, the tattered Villon approached and asked:
"The house you live in, how many doors has it?" and Dante
Took him aside, and grasping him by the sleeve, murmured:
"Your verses bristle with mistakes, my friend, think of all
                                   the enemies you've made!"
And from the other side Voltaire shouted:
"Look after your pennies or they'll starve you to death."
"And work a few jokes in," cried Heine. "It won't help,"
Shakespeare complained; "When James came, even I wasn't
                                   allowed to write."
"If they put you on trial, get a crook for your attorney,"
Advised Euripides, "He'll know the holes in the net of the law."
The laughter still resounded through the place when from
                                   the farthest corner
Came a cry: "You, newcomer! Do they know *your* verses by
                                   heart, too?
And those who do, will *they* escape persecution?"
"It is the forgotten," said Dante softly,
"Not only their bodies, their works, too, were destroyed."
The laughter broke off. None dared to look. The newcomer
Had turned pale.

105

Many of the poems Brecht wrote in the thirties are simply political, baldly social. But occasionally we catch a glimpse of the poet inside the politics. Here is Brecht on Easter Sunday, 1935.

### EASTER SUNDAY 1935
#### (*Ostersonntag*)

Early on this Easter Day
An impetuous snowstorm
Swept through the island;
Between the budding hedges lay snow.
My little son dragged me out
To see a little cherry tree
By the house wall;
From my writing table,
Where I was writing verses in which
I pointed at the men
Who were preparing a war
Which would destroy this island
And my people, and this continent of Europe,
And my family, and me.
Silently we placed a sack
Round the freezing tree.

OSTERSONNTAG

Eisler

Heu - te, O - ster - sonn - tag   früh, ging   ein plötz - li - cher

Schnee - sturm   ü - ber   die   In - sel,   zwi - schen den

grü - nen - den   Hek - ken   lag   Schnee.   Mein jun - ger

Sohn hol - te mich zu ei - nem A - pri - ko - sen - bäum - chen

an der Haus - mau - er von ei - nem Ver - se weg, in

dem ich auf die - je - ni - gen mit dem Finger deu - te - te,

die die - sen Krieg vor - be - rei - te - ten, der die - sen

Kon - ti - nent, die - se In - sel, mein Volk und mei - ne Fa -

mi - li - e und mich ver - til - - gen muss.

Schwei - gend leg - ten wir ei - nen Sack

um den frie - ren - den Baum.

This 1935 was the year also of the Nuremberg Laws, which among other things made a *Judenhure* of any German girl with a Jewish boyfriend.

### THE BALLAD OF MARIE SANDERS
*(Ballade von der Judenhure Marie Sanders)*

In Nuremberg they made a law
Giving women cause to weep
Who had been sleeping with the wrong man.
    The workers crouch in their tenements
    And hear the beating of drums.
    "God above, could there be something wrong tonight?
    Listen! Here it comes!"

Marie Sanders, does your boyfriend have raven hair?
If so, you better had make sure
This is the end of this affair.
    The workers crouch in their tenements
    And hear the beating of the drums.
    "God above, could there be something wrong tonight?
    Listen! Here it comes!"

Mother, give me the key please,
Everything will be all right.
The moon looks like it always did.
    The workers crouch in their tenements
    And hear the beating of the drums.
    "God above, could there be something wrong tonight?
    Listen! Here it comes!"

And at nine one morning she
Drove through the city in her slip
With a board round her neck,
Her head shaven,
The crowd jeering,
Her eyes cold.
    And thousands go down and line the streets,
    For Streicher's coming! Make room!
    God above, if they only used their ears
    They would know who does what and to whom!

## BALLADE VON DER JUDENHURE MARIE SANDERS

Eisler

In Nürnberg mach - ten sie ein Ge -

setz, dar - ü - ber wein - te man - ches Weib, das mit dem

fal - schen Mann im Bet - te lag. Das

Fleisch schlägt auf, in den Vor - städ - ten. Die

Trommeln schla - gen mit Macht. Gott im Him - mel,

wenn sie et - was vor - hät - ten, wär' es heu - te Nacht.

109

During the period of exile Brecht lived successively in Denmark, Sweden, and Finland. He has told what it felt like to listen to the German radio.

### TO THE LITTLE RADIO [6]
#### (*An den kleinen Radioapparat*)

O little box I carried in my flight
So as not to break the radio tubes inside me,
From house to boat, from boat to train, held tight,
So that my enemies could still address me
Right where I slept and much to my dismay,
Last thing at night, and first thing every day,
Announcing victories—defeats for me—
O please do not fall silent suddenly!

[6] Hanns Eisler's music for this lyric can be found in *Lieder und Kantaten* (Breit-kopf and Härtel Musikverlag, Leipzig, n.d.), 1, 110.

## AN DEN KLEINEN RADIOAPPARAT

Eisler

Du klei - ner Ka - sten, den ich flüch - tend trug, dass mei - ne Lam - pen mir auch nicht zer - brä - chen, be - sorgt vom Haus zum Schiff, vom Schiff zum Zug, dass mei - ne Fein - de wei - ter zu mir sprä - chen, an mei - nem La - ger und zu mei - ner Pein der letzten nachts, der er - sten in der Früh', von ih - ren Sie - gen und von mei - ner Müh. Versprich mir, nicht auf ein - mal stumm zu sein.

War came in 1939. Some of Brecht's war poetry is savage, for instance, the poem "To the German Soldiers in the East," the first of his poems that I translated. I would not care to reprint it today. The point is made less brutally in "The German Miserere."

### THE GERMAN MISERERE [7]
*(Das deutsche Miserere)*

Once upon a time our leaders gave us orders
To go out and conquer the small town of Danzig.
So we invaded Poland and with our tanks and bombers
We conquered all of Poland in a few days.

Once upon a time our leaders gave us orders
To go out and conquer the big town of Paris,
So we invaded France and with our tanks and bombers
We conquered all of France in a few days.

At a later date our leaders gave us orders
To conquer the moon and floor of the ocean,
And it's going badly with us in Russia
For the foe is strong and we're far from home.

God preserve us and lead us back again home!

[7] Hanns Eisler's music for this lyric is found in his *Lieder und Kantaten*, 1, 170.

## DAS DEUTSCHE MISERERE

*Nicht schleppen*                                                    Eisler

Ei - nes schö - nes Ta - ges be - fahl'n uns uns' - re O -

bern die klei - ne Stadt Dan - zig für sie zu er -

o - bern. Wir sind mit Tanks und Bom - bern in

Po - len ein - ge - bro - chen und ha - ben es er - o - bert

in zwei Wo - chen.

113

"Song of a German Mother" is so far from brutal that I have had letters from radio listeners asking: How could Brecht sympathize with a Nazi mother? The poem, of course, is not grounded in any such sympathy.

### SONG OF A GERMAN MOTHER
#### (*Lied einer deutschen Mutter*)

My son, I gave you the jackboots,
And the brown shirt came from me.
But had I known what I now know,
I'd have hanged myself from a tree.

And when I saw your arm, son,
Raised high in a Hitler salute,
I did not know that those arms, son,
Would wither at the root.

And then I saw you march off, son,
Following in Hitler's train,
And I did not know all those marchers
Would never come back again.

I saw you wear your brown shirt
And did not complain or entreat,
For I did not know what I now know:
It was your winding sheet.

## LIED EINER DEUTSCHEN MUTTER

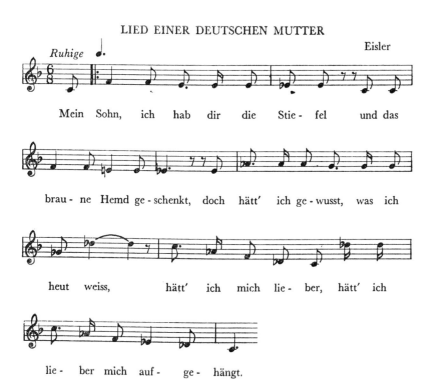

Eisler

*Ruhige*

Mein Sohn, ich hab dir die Stie - fel und das

brau - ne Hemd ge - schenkt, doch hätt' ich ge - wusst, was ich

heut weiss, hätt' ich mich lie - ber, hätt' ich

lie - ber mich auf - ge - hängt.

115

The poem "Homecoming," concerned with the end of the war, might also be called "Song of a German Son." In it, Brecht, still in America, contemplates his return to Augsburg.

### HOMECOMING [8]
#### (*Die Heimkehr*)

My father's town, what will it be like?
Following the swarms of bombers
I come back home.
And where is it? Yes, where is it?
Where those tremendous mountains of smoke are,
That's it, there! In the fire over there!
Father's town, how will it receive me now?
Before me come the bombers.
Deadly swarms announce to you my return.
Sheets of flame precede
Your son.

---

[8] Hanns Eisler's music to this lyric can be found in his *Lieder und Kantaten,* 1, 38.

### DIE HEIMKEHR

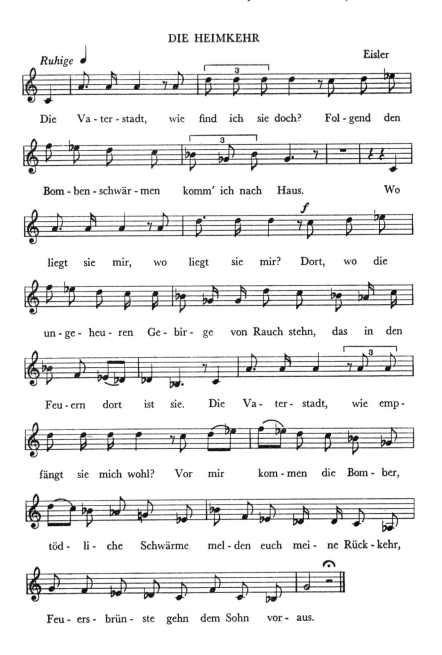

In 1947, still in this country, Bertolt Brecht appeared as a witness before the House Un-American Activities Committee. At the time he had in his pocket a plane ticket for Paris, and by 1949 he was a resident of the German Democratic Republic. In 1953, on the occasion of the revolt of June 17, he confirmed his loyalty to the Ulbricht regime. At the same time he wrote a poem which circulated, unpublished, much as his "Ballad of the Dead Soldier" had circulated during World War I. When a British journalist visited Professor Georg Lukacs in Budapest in 1961 and asked the Professor what he thought of the present situation, Lukacs reached for this poem of Brecht's and said: "Read!"

### THE SOLUTION
#### (*Die Lösung*)

After the rising of the seventeenth of June
The secretary of the Writers' Union
Had leaflets distributed on the Stalinallee
On which one could read that
The people had forfeited the confidence of the
                                        government
And could only win it back again by doing twice as
                                        much work.

Would it not be easier to
Dissolve the people and
Elect another?

Brecht's Communism was perhaps not quite wholehearted. Unequivocal, however, was his Pacifism. His radical attitude sprang in the first instance out of his experience in World War I. *Mother Courage* is a prophecy of World War II. And when East and West Germany began to rearm, Brecht made an antirecruiting play out of Farquhar's *The Recruiting Officer*. Brecht, in effect, appealed not only to West, but to East, Germans to avoid war.

## TO MY COUNTRYMEN
### (*An meine Landsleute*)

You who live on in towns that passed away,
Now show yourselves some mercy, I implore.
Do not go marching into some new war
As if the old wars had not had their day,
But show yourselves some mercy, I implore.

You men, reach for the trowel, not the knife.
Today you'd have a roof above your head
Had you not gambled on the knife instead,
And with a roof one has a better life.
You men, reach for the trowel, not the knife.

You children, that you all may stay alive,
Your fathers and your mothers you must waken
And if in ruins you would not survive,
Tell them you will not take what they have taken,
You children, that you all may stay alive.

You mothers, from whom all men take their breath,
A war is yours to give or not to give.
I beg you, mothers, let your children live!
Let them owe you their birth but not their death.
I beg you, mothers, let your children live!

I have violated chronology in order to save until the end a group of three short elegies collectively entitled, "To Those Who Come After." This group of poems combines the two Brechts, political and unpolitical, the believer and the sceptic. A presentation that begins with "About Poor B.B." should, I think, end with "To Those Who Come After."

## THREE ELEGIES [9]

### I

These are, indeed, dark times in which I live!
To say a guileless thing is foolish.
A smooth brow bespeaks insensitivity.
To laugh is to be someone who
Has not yet received the
Frightful news.

Times in which conversation about trees is almost a crime
Because it includes silence concerning atrocities,
What times these are!
That man there, calmly crossing the street,
Is he perhaps beyond the reach of friends in desperate need?

True, I still earn a living, but
That's an accident, believe me.
Nothing I do gives me the right to eat my fill.
I have been spared by chance.
If my luck gives out, I am lost.

Eat and drink, they tell me, be glad you have it!
But how can I eat and drink when
I take what I eat from someone who's hungry and when
Someone who's thirsty goes without my glass of water?
Yet I do eat and drink.

How I wish I were wise!
It's in old books what *wise* means.
To keep out of the world's strife,
To pass the short space without fear,
To survive without resort to violence,
To return good for evil,
Not to fulfill one's wishes but forget them:
This is what *wise* means.
All of which I cannot do.
These are, indeed, dark times in which I live.

---

[9] Hanns Eisler's music to this lyric can be found in his *Lieder und Kantaten*, I, 124, 191, 194.

II

I came to the cities in a time of disorder
When hunger reigned there.
I came among men in a time of revolt
And I rose up with the others.
So passed the time that was given me on earth.

I ate my food between battles.
I lay down to sleep among murderers.
I made love without enthusiasm
And looked upon Nature with impatience.
So passed the time that was given me on earth.

The roads in my time led into the swamp.
Speech betrayed me to the butcher.
I could do little. But without me
Rulers would have felt more secure, or so I hoped.
So passed the time that was given me on earth.

One's powers were slight. The goal
Lay in the far, far distance.
It was clearly visible if, also, for me,
Hardly to be reached.
So passed the time that was given me on earth.

### III

You,
You who will be borne up by the flood
In which we
Went down,
Remember, too,
When you speak of our weaknesses
The dark time
You have escaped:
How,
Changing our country more often than our shoes,
We walked through the wars of the classes
Despairing
When we saw injustice and no rebellion.

Yet this we knew:
Even hatred of baseness distorts the features.
Even anger at injustice makes the voice hoarse.
We, alas,
Who wished to prepare the ground for kindness
Could not ourselves be kind.

But you,
When things have reached the point where
Man is no wolf to man,
Remember us with
Forbearance.

# Index

139